A Love Quilt

Later Faith Patches

I dedicate this book to Mike Riddell, author, playwright, filmmaker, academic and Truth-speaker, with gratitude for friendship and his generous mentoring of the beginnings of
A Love Quilt: Later Faith Patches.

Someday,
after mastering the winds, the waves,
the tides and gravity,
we shall harness for God the energies of love,
and then, for a second time in the history of the world,
we humans will have discovered fire.

Pierre Teilhard de Chardin, (Adapted)

A Love Quilt

Later Faith Patches

Trish McBride

Philip Garside Publishing Ltd.

Copyright © 2020 and 2024 Trish McBride

All rights reserved.

This book or any portion thereof may not be reproduced or used in any manner whatsoever without the express written permission of the publisher except for the use of brief quotations in a book review.

Also by the author:
From the Shepherd's Mouth: A Study of Sexual Abuse in the Church, 1999

Faith Evolving: A Patchwork Journey, 2005, 2nd edition 2007,
3rd edition 2016, republished 2024

Exploring the Presence: More Faith Patches, 2011, republished 2024

Grateful thanks for permission to quote to:

Carol Christ, (personal permission)

Edwina Gateley, *Anointing* (personal permission)

Shirley Murray, verses of *A Place at the table*, (personal permission)

Enitharmon Press, publishers of UA Fanthorpe's *BC-AD,
Selected Poems and Christmas Poems*

Tui Motu InterIslands, for articles:
Mahboba, A Closure, Encountering Rumi, Hope and Healing in Prison, Living Wage;
and book review of *The Stardust Revolution*.

Republished 2024
International print-on-demand paperback edition:
ISBN 9781988572604

Also available:
New Zealand paperback: ISBN 9781988572567
USA print-on-demand paperback edition: ISBN 9798689743011
Kindle / Mobi eBook: ISBN 9781988572574
ePub eBook edition: ISBN 9781988572581
PDF eBook edition: ISBN 9781988572598

Philip Garside Publishing Ltd
PO Box 17160
Wellington 6147
New Zealand
books@pgpl.co.nz — www.pgpl.co.nz

Koru graphics sourced and adapted from:
www.vecteezy.com/free-vector/reflection

Front cover photograph:
Earth panel from the author's *Four Elements* quilt, 2006

Contents

Foreword 9

Introduction 11
    To the Unknown Woman 14

Being Loved 15
    Culture Shock 17
    Strange happenings 17
    Seeings 20
    Prayer of relationship: a personal journey 25
    Reluctance 31
    Easter Crossing 2000 32

Love and Creation 33
    Yatton Park 35
    Breath 37
    Wilton Bush 38
    Kākariki 38
    Osmosis 39
    Morning Praise 39
    Labyrinth 39
    The Bush 40
    In Spring 40
    Bee 40
    Learning 41
    Breakfast meditation 41
    Higher tide 42
    Down South 43
    The Stardust Revolution:
        The New Story of Our Origin in the Stars 45

Love and Community 47
- Spiritual Direction 49
- A True Story 50
- Rātana 52
- Mahboba's Promise 54
- Tibetan Journeys 56
- Gallipoli 62
- Encountering Rumi 62
- Words and Worship 64
- The Interfaith Journey 66
- The Pandemic 69

Love and Social Justice 73
- Pentecost Prayer 75
- Being A Neighbour 75
- Just Peace 77
- A Closure 79
- Sue's Tooth 81
- Stretching 82
- Listen, love, respect! Justice for Same-sex Couples 84
- The Living Wage Movement 89
- Abortion – A Middle Way? 92
- Hope and Healing in Prison 93
- Doing Racial Justice 96
- A Closer Look at Forgiveness 98

Love and Parish 109
- Ordination 111
- New Wineskins: Progressive Christianity 112
- Mysticism and Progressive Christianity 114
- A New Liturgical Season: Celebrating the Season of Creation 117
- Storm Reflection 124
- Storm Prayer 125

Humanity Reflection	126
Good Friday	128
New Year Reflection, 2017	129
Light	130
Ponderings	**131**
Jesus and Evolution	133
Musings on Metaphors	135
Letting Go	137
Bad Back	139
Mortality	140
Am I a Christian?	142
Blessing	145
Endnotes	146
Bibliography	148
Periodicals	150
Websites	150
Glossary	151
Acknowledgements	153
About the Author	154
About the Book	154
Praise for A Love Quilt	155
Books by Trish McBride	156

Foreword

Surely one of the most privileged experiences has to be listening to or reading the spiritual journey of another person. Almost always we find ourselves responding in at least three ways, all of which are true of me as I read *A Love Quilt: Later Faith Patches.* Given that this is a contribution to spiritual autobiography, describing the work of the inner quest and the process of discovery of the true self written by a woman about my age and background, as expected I identified deeply in parts of it, especially with writers like Carol Christ, Edwina Gately and Rumi, and events such as the charismatic renewal that have been part of my own story. Then I realised that I was fascinated by Trish's uniqueness, things she has lived through that are not my experience, but which have deeply formed this woman Trish who invites us into conversation with her narrative and reflections. Finally I cherished the whole context in which she is writing, this Aotearoa which is so beautiful (as described in her trip "Down South") and yet so broken (as I hear again in her writing the call to racial, economic and gender justice).

Trish's commitment in writing is to share, consider and wonder about the blessing of Divine Love that has been her life (so far!). She does this in beautiful evocative language, with questions about living deeply that linger: "When you say 'worship' what do you mean?" "How do we nurture emerging paradigms of Christianity?" "What would Jesus, the Compassion of God, want for those damaged by others?" The latter is within one of the most challenging sections of the book. But there is more that some might find tough, especially – in very different ways – the intellectual confronting of the inter-spirituality section and the heartbreak of the story of Mana Recovery. Images at times both startle and comfort, such as the picture of the friends gathered at a funeral as a body giving birth to the loved one.

This is a profoundly inner story but definitely not a solitary one. Trish has peopled it with insightful companions, like The Unknown Woman, Jacob Berkowitz, Bridget and James, Mahboba, Paula, Shirley and John, David Bohm and many others, some of whom will be known to readers but they appear here as her teachers and friends. The experiences are very wide-ranging and deeply human.

There is some poetry written by others but most of it is her own as she contemplates events and happenings that have touched her profoundly. I look forward to using some of this in my own spiritual direction work, as the experiences are both individual and universal. There are resources too, notably *The Land Sunday Service* and *The Storm Reflection*, which others may find helpful in various faith communities to develop insight, commitment, resilience.

This is the story of the faith patches that make up the later stages of one woman's spiritual life. You too may indeed identify with and discover anew, but you will not find this book mundane or prescriptive or even the end of the journey. Trish ends with a brief and beautiful blessing: may her writing bring rich blessing to you and those with whom you share it. Thank you, Trish, for trusting us with the mystery and multi-layered fabric pieces of your later life.

Rev Dr Jenny Dawson, August 2020

Introduction

Love is the prime component of life: attraction, connection, commitment, generativity. It has been so since the Big Bang as the primal atom components first connected, then formed molecules, and is so still. I'd no idea, when I first gathered a few writings together as a possible book, that Divine Love would emerge as the overall theme, or that aspects and implications of the receiving and giving would flow into patterns for the quilt I had in mind.

Divine Love. Where to start? Two points spring to mind. One is the human need to feel loved, and our capacity to be our best selves when we have that confidence and want to live in response. The other is the many varieties of faith journeys, including those of the heart and those of the head. There are those who find their primary experiences of the sacred through nature and the goodness of humanity, those for whom the sacred is encountered primarily through the internal spiritual experience of relationship with the Divine, and those for whom the intellect is the primary way. These, of course, are not water-tight compartments, they flow together in us all, merge, and separate again like the streams of one of our braided rivers. But we each have our natural calling to one or other of these modes. Mid-life balancing means developing our wider possibilities.

We each recognise the sacred in our own experience in our unique way because we are all different. Our journeys and theologies are necessarily grounded in our own experience. In the Christian tradition, as well as other faith traditions, we have the age-old strands of the theological and the contemplative or mystical. I believe passionately that there is a need for loving and respectful communication between these strands. They need each other if Christianity is to survive in its wholeness. 'Yes' to the rigorous integration of science and theology, and 'yes' to the acknowledgement of the experiential contemplative or mystical path. Christianity would never have lasted 2,000 years if there was no experiential impact.

Somewhere in my 30s I said to God, 'They keep saying you love me, but it's not much use if I can't tell!' I've written my way through my experiences of that Divine Love since then and my attempts to live its implications. So here with that theme is *A Love Quilt: Later Faith Patches*, the third book of quilted patches, writings of Life and Faith fabric stitched together, as were *Faith Evolving: A Patchwork Journey* (2005) and *Exploring the Presence: More Faith Patches* (2011).

In 2003 I had no intention of writing a book, let alone a trilogy covering most of 70 years. When I heard there were no longitudinal studies of how the thinking and practice of many Christian women changed over an extended period, I realised I had 30 years' worth of prose and poetry stashed away, beginning from the 1970s. When chronologically arranged, these recorded life events and challenges, my feminist awakening, re-thinking of handed-on faith, departure from my Catholic roots and subsequent several years with the Quakers. Life events included our six children and foster daughter, my husband's sadly alcoholic life and early death, sexual abuse as a new widow, solo parent and employee by a Methodist minister, and the beginnings of healing from all that. I experienced God's love in some very tangible personal ways during these experiences. In that first book, I used Fowler's Stages of Faith and Myers Briggs Personality Type Indicators (MBTI) to provide some analysis of the shifts in my understanding and theology. Hence *Faith Evolving*.

Exploring the Presence is a more varied collection of writings, covering times before and after its predecessor. By 2011, I had given up on church connections but a hermit-like Christ-centred spiritual journey was still my life axle. I explored far and wide, both geographically and spiritually, for instance the wonderful Goddess Pilgrimage to Crete in 2006, and a Shamanic workshop in 2009, as well as learning from the recognised major faiths. I was learning to translate differently named concepts and dynamics from other spiritual frameworks into comparable Christian language and recognising so many striking similarities between them and my own heritage. This book, unsurprisingly, proved too pagan for the Christians and too Christian for the pagans.

A Love Quilt: Later Faith Patches is a further collection, written in what could be called old age. It is actually the happiest and most tranquil time of my life, despite occasional turmoil and grief. I re-connected with a formal church in 2012, after realising that St Andrew's on The Terrace, Wellington, a Progressive Presbyterian parish, was communally living the basic principles of my faith: Social Justice practised internally, including the use of inclusive language, the valuing of diversity and women's ministry. While holding to my post-denominational stance, I have been able occasionally to lead services and otherwise serve with the ministry training I've acquired over the last 30 plus years. I'd long felt a call to priestly ministry but that simply couldn't happen in the Catholic context.

For about 40,000 years, our fore-mothers have stitched things together and shared skills and resources. They started with skins and bone awls. They connected pieces of skins and plant, and later wove to create clothes, coverings, and shelter. This is the tradition I call on again in *A Love Quilt*, as I stitch together pieces of my learning and thinking from the last decade or so, including my evolving image of God. And maybe this book is the binding together for the bigger quilt of all my life themes and stories. The central story is the blessing of Divine Love which I have experienced in so many privileged and astonishing ways, and my attempts to live out its implications.

As these pieces were written over the last decade for assorted contexts and none, there are some necessary repetitions. Rather than irritate, these will hopefully underline my main themes of Life in Love and Faith as I have known it.

The book's first piece is about a literal quilt. The poem tells the story of a life's work which had been discarded when its creator had left it unfinished. I was privileged to come across it and give it the time and reverence it deserved. Some of its central fabrics date back to the 1940s – the decade of my birth. I trimmed away the messy outer edges and gave it substance and a backing. It is now completed, beautiful and much honoured. She would have loved it! Would she have finished it herself if eyes and life had lasted longer? Is all our life work ultimately 'unfinished'? Perhaps to be given some significance and completed by others? What else might happen if we had more years than our reality? Her work became a treasured quilt, which like Life, was not a solo performance – so many contribute to our life stories in so many ways, both seen and unseen.

That quilt's story parallels the way this book is written: her patches were fabrics that would have been drawn from many sources – family scraps and those contributed by many friends. My life patches could not have become a lived reality in isolation. Each draws on all the wonderful people who are and have been gifts in my life: family, friends, spiritual directors, teachers, therapists, other writers and thinkers, those who published some of my pieces in other contexts, which gave me confidence they may have something to offer a wider readership. The God who, permeating All that Is, draws me on towards my completion: the time when I'm required to relinquish all the borrowed atoms that make up my physical frame, and return them to Mother Earth, to the Cosmos.

The quilt metaphor has wider possibilities. My life patches in this book quilt, while differently shaded and textured, have all been co-woven with the Weaver of Life on the great Loom of the Cosmos. And an even wider application: each human, each other element in existence is a patch of the Universal Quilt. How we choose to attach and relate to all other 'patches' has a vital part to play in the whole creative venture. Strong joinings make a strong Quilt.

As with my earlier books, a secondary purpose is to document some threads of Christian thinking in the 2000s. The primary purpose of them all is to encourage you, the reader, to reflect on the happenings and ponderings of your own life, your own life quilt. Tell, record your own stories of inner and outer journeys – they are important. Carol Christ's words quoted at the beginning of *Faith Evolving* are still pertinent and encouraging:

> 'The expression of women's spiritual quest is integrally related to the telling of women's stories. If women's stories are not told, the depths of women's souls will not be known.'

So herewith some stories, poems and ponderings.

To the Unknown Woman

Raggy five-dollar bundle
awe and reverence
as it unfolded
and unfolded and unfolded
huge work of patient care
this work of pieced-together years

Woman of patience and perseverance,
who were you?
that year after year
after year
you cut placed sewed together
with minute stitches
fabrics from your dresses,
your friends' your children's
and maybe their children's too
year after year
hexagon by hexagon
decade after decade
growing … growing … growing

What was the plan, the hope?
a quilt for your double bed?
but he didn't come back
for your daughter's?
but they split up
for your grand-daughter's?
but she didn't want Nan's
old-fashioned stuff

Year after year, piece by piece
until eyes gave out
stitching too hard
edges got messy
fingers no longer worked
sad and tired
you bundled it into a drawer
to be found by those
who later cleared your home
and with barely a pang
packed all those years
of tranquil work
off to the op shop

I've finished your quilt
your long-time companion
and see it happily treasured now
in a home whose birthdate
maybe matched your own
I honour your work and think of you
with love!

Being Loved

Being Loved

In this section are records of key moments of my personal journey, deep experiences of being loved and taught by God/Jesus several decades ago, and my subsequent ponderings. There were many other times – occasionally the Voice, startling provision of financial resources in the earlier times of poverty, and assorted 'synchronicities.'

Culture Shock

Strange dark hill of pines
hangs over strange brick school
no grass no bikes
the nuns all look the same
we wear slippers inside
they polish the floors after school
and want us to be nuns too
to prove we love God enough

> For my last year at school I attended St Mary's College in Wellington. After Tauranga College, it was very alien. I did feel called to religious life – but instead took the path of marriage and family.

Strange happenings

Through my life as a deeply involved Christian, I've had some physical experiences that were at the times astonishing and inexplicable. I'll describe three of these – two were not then obviously connected with anything spiritual. In retrospect, they fuelled my interest in the common ground between psychology and spirituality. I wondered much later what had been happening at a cellular/neurological level.

> Many people have unusual physical responses to situations. Mostly they get set aside and forgotten, but maybe there is some significance to be discovered.

At a school friend's sixteenth birthday party, someone suggested we 'play spirits' – a totally new concept to me, and well before I heard this was a 'not ok' thing for Christians to do. So we had the letters round the table and the wine glass with our fingers on its upturned base. It buzzed around, satisfactorily spelling words as the others asked questions, and this seemed quite magical. Then when it spelled out an answer to a question plus an unusual comment, I recognised that this response had earlier been in my mind – word for word – but wasn't at that immediate time. Could it be that something of me was influencing what happened? Very weird! Then I experimented with formulating answers, carefully didn't push the glass, and lo and behold, my thoughts, conscious now, were played out in the answers. I told no-one but surmised that there is a power in human beings that doesn't have a name. Then I forgot about it for decades.

When I was fairly new to Catholic Charismatic Renewal in the 1970s, I had received Baptism in the Spirit and was happy enough praying in the previously-dreaded tongues. I was encouraged to join the group in laying on hands as a prayer for healing for someone. As we prayed, there was an enormous charge of energy down through my head, body and arms which literally nearly knocked me over. Scary stuff! Was God that involved in our lives and prayers? The others reassured me that this sort of thing can happen. For a few years whenever I laid hands on someone, there could be a lesser charge and the person would say, 'I felt that!' 'God doing something' was the communal interpretation.

The most dramatic time was towards the end of my years-long psychotherapy. Laura, my therapist, had been away for three weeks. I felt I was within a short while of finishing the work but had really missed her. The first session after she came back, I said something, now no idea what, and she suddenly said she had to stop working with me but would do the couple of months to the end of the year. I was beside myself with bewilderment, shock and grief, and later that day went for a massage. As my belly was worked on, I could feel a huge snake in my pelvis working its way up through my body. The massage stopped. I was in huge pain and said it was like having a baby, but it was pushing up not down, breaking through something on the way. I was retching and terrified but was eventually able to settle and go home. I rang Laura in the night. She said it was the retrieval of the true self. It was a couple of days before I was fully recovered.

This matched absolutely nothing in my experience, framework or vocabulary. No Charismatic elements fitted. I thought I should feel somehow different after such an enormous experience but didn't. Early the next year I attended a university Religious Studies course on mysticism across faiths and cultures. I was deeply shocked to hear a Hindu description of kundalini as a snake rising through the body as a manifestation of spiritual energy. I'd never heard of this but it matched what had happened. A few months later, I was still in pain and grief, and one night I felt something physically realign, like a joint going back into a socket. Then I got (or received?) a transformation – the next morning all the colours of the world shone brightly, and I felt deeply renewed. Months later again, it dawned on me that the feelings I'd had on Laura's 'desertion' were the feelings I hadn't been allowed, aged 4, on my mother's 'desertion' to tend the new baby and my war-damaged father on his return home. So deeply buried, and now released.

Because a friend was writing the end of her own therapy story, I mentioned my presumed kundalini time. She wrote back asking if I knew Dorothy Walters, an expert and writer on this experience. I'd never heard of her, so Googled and watched an hour's interview between her and an Andrew Harvey, and phew! so much in common, even though my 'snake' happening was very different from theirs. A startling physical experience leading to the joy of newly knowing God's Love. Andrew talked about being plugged into a socket too. They talked about the Sufi Islamic poet Rumi – he is very important in my life – and also mentioned the medieval Beguine mystic Hadewich. I've long loved those medieval women mystics.

A recent read told the same story of the same sort of experience coming via yoga. Seane Corn's book *Revolution of the Soul* describes her journey from the depths of drugs and prostitution, through gradual growth in awareness along with internal physical happenings, to experiencing what she too describes as God's Love and her consequent service to the world.

It's tragic that so much emphasis in Christian teaching has been about observance and reward after death, but not on the unearned gift of experiencing transformation, the human wholeness, offered us in this life. I've been blessed with Catholic and other teachers and guides who did know this. Our Christian understanding of God and the gift of Divine Love is exactly what Rumi, Dorothy, Andrew and Seane were talking about. Christianity does not have a monopoly of this experience. It comes to those of many faiths and none. This transforming gift does not mean learning or challenges are over. It marks an important point in the journey – but is not a once-and-for-always resolution. There has been, and still is, much more to do. I know that depth Christianity has brought me to this place, and that depth spirituality and depth psychology are two sides of the same coin.

About 20 years ago, after pondering the point, I figured the ultimate purpose of the Christian Church is to lead or coach or draw each individual into the experience of God's Love. A few weeks later I was startled to see Pope John Paul II had made the same statement. As I was well out of the Catholic fold by then and disagreed with a lot he'd had to say over the years, this was an interesting moment. My corollary is that the meaning and purpose of human life is to learn to love. Much easier when we have had our own experiences of being loved. The evangelists did their best to relay this in the Christian Scriptures, but so much has got lost along the way. 'We love because God first loved us.' 1 John 4:19. 'God is Love' 1 John 4:8.

Rumi is the one who sums it up for me:

Love is the Treasure

The temple of love is not love itself;
True love is the treasure, not the walls about it.
Do not admire the decoration
But involve yourself in the essence,
The perfume that invades and touches you,
The beginning and the end
Discovered, this replaces all else
The apparent, the unknowable.
Time and space are slaves to this presence.

Seeings

> Here are brief accounts of my life-healing and life-shaping times of interaction with Jesus.

Many people in the Christian tradition have moments of deep experience of Divine Love in their lives. Why else would the whole tradition have lasted for 2000 years? I had several life-giving and life-changing experiences which took place over about a decade from 1984. They left me astounded, awed and feeling deeply loved. Gifts and lessons are always given for sharing with the community, so here is an acknowledgement of the most memorable and dramatic visual occasions, of encounters with Jesus. In each I was fully present in the moment as the interactions unfolded. Three happened spontaneously and four were initiated through an initial imagination exercise. Most were described in various forms in my earlier books, referenced as *Faith Evolving* (FE) and *Exploring the Presence* (EP). The memories and their effects sustained me through further hard times. I now live joyfully with the outcome of it all. The lessons I was taught are for all of us.

The first occasion was in 1984. At the time, as well as being awed, I was also scared. This stuff wasn't meant to happen to ordinary people. That's when I first decided to seek spiritual direction. A recent poem sums it up:

Surrender

She saw him crucified
He whispered, 'I'm thirsty.'
Distraught, she asked
'What can I do for you?'
He replied
'It's you I'm thirsty for.'
She said 'Here I am.'

It was many years before I recognised the generosity of his use of the 'thirst' image, given our family situation.

The lesson: I am valued, wanted. So are we all.

A 1986 retreat experience, also involving the crucifixion, was a gift that cracked a shell. It started with a reflection suggested by the retreat director on the story of the woman who washed Jesus' feet. I truly couldn't myself as a sinner, had never been able to. I'd avoided guilt by doing what was required of me and couldn't understand why it was not so easy and simple for others.

As I prayed with the suggested scripture, I asked Jesus what part my self-righteousness had played in his crucifixion. Again, I saw Jesus on the cross. His reply: 'Your self-righteousness is the nails that fasten my hands and feet when I want to walk through your life to touch and heal.' (FE 70) That sorted me!

> The lesson: Energy put into 'being good' can get in the way of an emotionally honest relationship.

The next occasion was as I prayed on my bed at home one afternoon. This time was also life-changing. I think it was in 1987. I found myself paralysed in a hospital bed. Jesus came as the nurse with bowl and towel, offering to give me my wash. It was a hugely embarrassing struggle to accept, but I did, and was tenderly washed with love and told how beautiful I was. Afterwards, quite shocked, I thought of Peter objecting to having just his feet washed! I wondered later about my body image before this, that it needed such drastic healing. I hadn't really disliked my body; it was just largely ignored – it was something that kept my head off the floor. (FE 81)

> The lesson: My body deserves reverence. All bodies do!

In maybe 1988 I sensed a change in my prayer – the old way didn't seem to be working anymore. There was a bewildering array of other ways to do it, of books on how to find God. I told my spiritual director about the confusion I was feeling. 'Have you talked to Jesus about how you feel?' she asked.

I hadn't, of course, but went away to do so not sure what, if anything, this would accomplish. 'Jesus,' I said, feeling slightly foolish, 'I'm pretty confused about how to pray right now. It's like standing at a crossroads with a dozen roads all sign-posted to God. I don't have a clue which one to take'. Suddenly I had a sense of Jesus standing beside me at the crossroads saying, 'Hold my hand, close your eyes, and I will take you the way that's right for you.' So I did. I was awed by the new understanding of being involved in a unique relationship, that there was a call to go on in trust, that I would be guided, that all would be well. And so, it is still.

> The lesson: We each have our individual ways to be met and led by the Holy.

I was on retreat again with the same spiritual director, several years after my husband died in 1986. She suggested I go in prayer with Jesus to meet him. I'd already done a lot of therapy and spiritual direction work around resolving our suddenly-ended difficult relationship. So I was reluctant, but chose to follow the suggestion and was gob-smacked by the power of interactions between the three of us and the reconciliation that took place. (FE 71)

Since then I've had a real faith that there is an after-life, that people are enlightened after death, that they welcome continued relationship, and that any needed healing can come. Which altogether fitted a grief counselling expert's talk years later on the concept of Continuing Bonds with the departed ones.[1]

> The lesson: Relationships continue beyond the grave.

In 1992, there was the most cosmic and belief-changing experience of all. A friend was dying. I was angry. I shouted, 'Where are you, God?' And suddenly I saw the words

'I AM HERE', in multiple versions, moving gently and purposefully in one direction through all that is – the Cosmos, the rocks and trees, through people, through myself. It was, I discovered later, something like early computer 'wall-paper', though at the time I had never seen anything like that. It convinced me of the All-pervading Presence and Activity, way before I'd read any quantum science or watched Brian Swimme's DVDs *The Powers of the Universe*. The poem was written at the time and appears in the two earlier books.

Presence

Where are you, God?
And then the words
Words within and words without –
I am here

A resonance that permeates, pervades
A whisper echoing through the universe
A song in the depths of my being –
I am here

Words of love, words of joy
Consoling words, creation words
Nowhere unspoken –
I am here

Burning bush that startles
Fine edged sword that knows
No boundaries of skin or heart –
I am here

Glimpse of simple sentence
Stretched through time
Reassurance of sustaining –
I am here

Effervescent words, ineluctable words
Indwelling, inebriating words
Silent words dancing words –
I am here

And I caught up in the dance
Am present to the All in all!

The lesson: All is One, truly infused with Divine Presence. (FE 59 & EP 145)

At a spiritual directors' training course in 1993, we were led on a guided meditation: 'Go to a special place and meet Jesus there'. I've always loved waterfalls and feel an extra delight when a rainbow shimmers in the spray. So there I was, in a place like that, and Jesus came hopping across the rocks, to meet me, smiling happily. That much was my intentional imagining. The rest simply and astonishingly happened. On the way over, he paused to collect the rainbow over his arm. Then when he reached me, he tenderly draped it round me as a sari, and pressed a red dot to my forehead. Such exquisite awe! I felt very loved. As previously, I did not understand the significance at the time. I painted an unskilled picture of the encounter – not that I was going to forget it! Later I was interested in his use of Hindu symbols. Much later again, I discovered that the bindi or tika could be a sign of marriage, of receiving the third eye of wisdom. In 2006 I visited the church of St Gregory of Nyssa in San Francisco and was startled to see a huge fresco of the marriage of Jesus and the Soul, very similar to my little painting, just no waterfall and with a presiding Mother-in-law God. And one day in 2009 during a hard time, there was a rainbow in the sky and I heard him remind me, 'Here is your sari.'

The lesson: I am cherished! We all are! (EP 162)

Reflection

As since those times my theology has evolved, and as I have discovered more of the depth of the human psyche, I have wondered what was going on in my brain during those experiences. I've read theories of the possibility of epilepsy, and of their simply arising from the personal unconscious. Neither of those rings true. They were so enormously not me! Especially in therapy, I've had stuff come up from my unconscious, been startled, but have recognised whatever it was as coming from my own depths. Epilepsy doesn't fit either. What I have deduced is that the combination of my significantly stressful life situation, a fairly intense spiritual practice and personality type may have facilitated these gifts of amazing healing encounters. But still the question 'Why me?' When I first heard the oft-repeated analysis 'the Jesus of history and the Christ of faith,' I wondered to myself 'But what about the Jesus of experience?' And the question Jesus/God as therapist?

My introduction to MBTI was enlightening and very freeing. INFJs – Introversion, Intuition, Feeling, and Judgment – (1% of the population) 'have an unusually rich inner life', 'are likelier to experience ESP, have a better understanding of psychic phenomena, are vulnerable to the eruption of their own archetypal material, find conflict extremely destructive to their psyches' (*Please Understand Me*, Keirsey and Bates). And 'The INFJ's are apt to have experiences of God's love and presence which bring new, deep insights into some aspect of religion or sacred Scripture.' (*Prayer and Temperament*, Michael and Norrisey)

So thankfully all that information confirmed for me that these experiences were pure unearned gift, and to some extent an accident of birth or genetics. They began when I was a member of a Charismatic covenant community where such things were not unusual, and continued through the most stressful period of my life. I honestly thought that sort of thing happened to everyone who prayed. Discovering that wasn't the case was somewhat bewildering. I was already in 1998 wondering whether Jesus was somehow connected to archetypes, so I wrote him a letter asking about various questions I was pondering at the time. (FE 118) Here is the relevant extract:

Dear Jesus,

> …Jung was convinced that the spiritual dimension was the key to almost all the emotional and psychological problems of his patients. He also introduced us to the world of archetypes. Those shadowy but immensely powerful images inhabit the deep realms within each of us, inviting and challenging us to greater wholeness – to the abundant life that you promised to give us. When I read a book about archetypes the list made for profound thought: the divine child, the creator, the magician, the joker/trickster, the saviour, the lover, the care-giver, the wise king and others. What really intrigued me was the thought that all these archetypes are somehow or other found in you, in the stories we have about your life on earth, in the titles we give you. Is this the real significance of your 'laying down your life' and your Divinity? That in and through you we are able to access whatever archetypes we need to become complete? When you come in prayer to startle and heal, is this the same phenomenon that is experienced by those who also encounter archetypes, say, in their dreams?…

Morton Kelsey, priest and Jungian analyst, has a diagram of the psyche as a triangle with a dotted line at the base to represent the permeability of the personal unconscious. This makes sense to me. If our unconscious can be infiltrated by Jung's collective unconscious, then Holy Mystery has an even greater capacity to speak through that and be creative within us.

I began working with a spiritual director because I was so shaken and scared by the first happening. Several wise ones over 30 years have accompanied and guided me through. Each profound experience was acknowledged in that context as it happened, but this is the first time I have put them all together. A necessary and sacramental grounding after the experiences was my later long-term work with the psychotherapist, because there the healings of the prayer experiences were earthed, grounded by a fully accepting human relationship. She said she was 'non-spiritual' and a 'non-believer' but described her practice as 'based on agape,' the highest form of love.

The lessons and the Love go on. Whatever the actual dynamics of the experiences, they were extraordinary, healing, humbling and life-shaping. They have gone on reverberating through the years as different layers of significance revealed themselves. For these and the many other times of astonishment, I give thanks. And offer them to fellow pilgrims who may find healing, encouragement and Love there for their own journeys. Whatever meanings these stories of mine hold for anyone else, all prayer that holds healing and a life-giving experience is an encounter with Divine Mystery.

Prayer of relationship: a personal journey

For me prayer happens within a relationship. In any deep human relationship, there is an almost infinite variety of communication styles, from 'please pass the butter' to deep and wordless communion. And along that spectrum, crucially, there's the honest sharing of thoughts and feelings. It can be like that in our communication with the Holy One, with Jesus. And because we are all different, each communication process will be different. Goddess/God is infinitely willing and able to relate to each of us in a way that's unique to each one. But we can only be our limited human selves in this relationship as fully and authentically as we can, with awareness that this will change over time.

> This was my contribution to one of a series of Catholic theology books, *Journeying into Prayer: People and their Pathways* (2012). Since then prayer has evolved with far fewer words.

Three formative influences on my prayer have been a childhood prayer-book, a lengthy Charismatic phase, and spiritual direction, receiving it for over 25 years, and training to offer this ministry myself over 20 years ago.

Childhood Prayer

An English Sister wove the web of words that captured me when I was six and holds me still – a series of scripture reflections, which laid the foundation of prayer. Jesus tells a Gospel story to the child-heart, describing his experiences and what he wants the child to learn.

> 'Little child, do not be deceived by the world and its poor play-toys, nothing is real but God, there is nobody nor anything that can give you happiness. Only here will you find it… You can tell me all your little secrets and I shall tell you mine.'

So in the beginning of my conscious prayer-life were words I believed, that had Jesus wanting my love and attention, wanting me to talk to him, and waiting to respond to me. I am grateful to that unknown Sister. She lit the fuse of something crucial. In retrospect, it is wonderful that in an age when Catholics weren't supposed to read the Bible, she was introducing a profound method of scriptural prayer called lectio divina (divine reading). She introduced me to a Jesus who was all Love, with whom dialogue was normal and to be expected, a human friend who took me seriously and wanted to understand me. This relationship has endured and matured ever since.

Charismatic Renewal

For many years I belonged to the Catholic Charismatic movement, and many important learnings from then are still with me. My early attendance at the weekly prayer group was sporadic. After an absence of a few months I arrived one night to discover it was the first evening of a Life in the Spirit Seminar. Baptism and Confirmation had already endowed me with the Holy Spirit. Do you want to know God in a new way? How could I say 'no' to that? I'd had a sense that there had to be more to it all than I already knew. Within six weeks I too was praying in tongues and raising my arms in prayer. And the first time I, with the group, laid hands on someone to pray for healing, a charge of power through me to the person we were praying for nearly knocked me off my feet, physically, spiritually and intellectually. No-one had ever told me God did stuff like that. God right there, God involved with us in unthinkable ways.

Over the next years there were many such experiences, always awesome but becoming less astounding. And there were the dreams. The first one introduced me to Scripture in a new way. I had woken unable to remember anything of it except the odd sounding reference of Daniel, chapter 2, verse 4. What did that mean? Could it be something in the Bible? Daniel doesn't often figure in the liturgy, so I didn't even know there was such a book. I pulled Grandma's old Douay Bible off the shelf, gave it a much-needed dust and looked in the index. And there indeed was Daniel. Found the reference, then just laughed because it was about this king who'd had a funny dream, then woke but couldn't remember what it was all about. This was obviously not a coincidence. What was God telling me? That He (because that's how it was then) was willing and able to communicate through the Word? That too re-organised both head and faith.

We were committed to giving God prime place in our lives, and discovered that faithfully practised prayer facilitates personal experiences of God's love and healing. We related to all three members of the Trinity, loved, studied and responded to the Word of God, and accepted the responsibility to be in ministry that was imparted by our baptism. We became open to sharing faith and worship with people from other Christian denominations and appreciated the Jewish roots of and influences on the Catholic/Christian Church.

Spiritual Direction
I have received and given spiritual direction for many years. A trained Christian person helps another to pay attention to God's personal communication to her/him, to respond to and grow in intimacy with God, and live out the consequences of this relationship. Traditionally this Catholic practice was for and by clergy and religious. But since the 1980s it has been embraced by many denominations and is now widely available to ordinary lay people who want to develop their prayer life, and perhaps train in this ministry. There is a professionally-focused national association,[2] international links and a strong trans-denominational ethos. Regular, probably monthly, face-to-face meetings are best but phone, email and sometimes Skype are also possible.

The various wise people who have had this role in my life have accompanied me in finding a workable way to pray through the complexities of my life. (See also the story about meeting Jesus at the crossroads in the *Seeings* section, p 20.)

Over the years, I've learned how to use for myself and others a matrix that includes personality typing (Myers Briggs, Enneagram), Fowler's Stages of Faith, dream-work, visualisations etc. It was a revelation and a relief to discover that INFJs like me have huge difficulty with repetitive prayer (the Rosary) and with prayers in other people's words unless they are an exact fit. And yes, that's how it's been, to the point where I stopped being able to attend communal Catholic liturgies. The necessary shift for me to imaging the Holy One as feminine added to my pain and discomfort with traditional services such as Mass, for so long the mainstay of life and prayer. When one can no longer say the Lord's Prayer or the Creed there's a significant problem! All language for the Divine is metaphor, but the metaphors generated by my inmost being are rejected by the institution. And vice versa. Another big shift was asking what She wanted 'for' me, rather than 'from' me, to Goddess/God as Friend.

These three influences remain. Recently two university Religious Studies courses and reading have given me tools for the beginnings of scientific understanding of the non-normal psychic or psychological phenomena in spiritual life, the religious experiences so ordinary to most of us in the prayer-group back then, and so appreciated. They occur in other faith traditions too. Neurologists and others have researched the physical, emotional and mental processes and benefits of faith, prayer and meditation.[3] It makes sense to me now that fervent prayer for solutions to difficulties can change brain function, open cells to receive, rather than getting God to change 'His' mind. This makes the Creative Power at work in us more rather than less awesome.

An Inter-spirituality Retreat

At the beginning of 2010 I took part in an email retreat where daily reflections on a weekly theme arrived from teachers of five world religions[4] (including Rev Cynthia Bourgeault, a recent visitor to New Zealand), and I was struck by the many similarities between the others and the Christian Way. I met there the term 'inter-spirituality' as a way to describe sharing practice – a deeper level than the possibly more cognitive 'interfaith'. I then went to a Buddhist Goddess Retreat, loved what we did. We noted that maybe half the participants were from a Catholic background. We saw correspondences between Buddhist and Catholic symbolisms and teaching. An involved Catholic layman there suggested an interfaith retreat, and I tweaked the word to 'inter-spirituality'. With the support of another Christian spiritual director and an organiser/accounts person, we held the retreat in April 2011. We called it Coming to the Heart, a concept important in many traditions.

People from seven world faith traditions gathered at the Home of Compassion in Island Bay to share with each other contemplative/meditative practices related to Compassion, which is ground common to all. Eighteen people attended, from Shamanic, Hindu, Daoist, Buddhist, Jewish, Christian and Sufi traditions. The  presenters were all approached by personal contact – no-one was there as "official" representative of their tradition. We provided an empty kete (basket), a framework into which they could bring treasures from their own tradition for sharing. The

Home of Compassion was spiritually and physically an ideal setting. It was a very enriching time for everyone, and a small piece in the jigsaw of world peace. We had heard along the way that Spiritual Directors International had also arranged an interfaith gathering on Compassion that same weekend in Atlanta, Georgia, so both gatherings acknowledged each other as being part of a bigger Spirit-led picture. Other denominations and groups locally and globally are currently working with Karen Armstrong's Charter for Compassion. A significant movement of the Spirit!

We began on the Friday evening with introducing ourselves and giving an overview of our connection with our tradition. And with some good silence together, we initiated the personal relationships that became the locus of our unity, of Compassion.

The format for Saturday and Sunday morning was that one to three presenters had 90 minutes to introduce their tradition, offer us all a practice/meditation/activity relating to Compassion to share, and for questions and discussion with the group. Everyone was generous in their sharing, courageous in trust, and we were rewarded by a new range of understandings of other traditions and appreciation for faith-at-work in each other. There was a shamanic journey, a Hindu chanting meditation, a Daoist meditation and tai chi, a Buddhist visualisation/meditation, the Jewish ritual to end the Sabbath and four levels of scripture reflection, a Christian invitation to let our hearts be touched by nature, a lesson in Sufi turning (whirling dervishes) and a breathing meditation.

We had a centre table on which symbols from all the traditions were placed. It was a wonderful array including a cross from Iona, a menorah, a bundle of feathers, Ganesh, figurines of a Sufi turner and an old Chinese man doing Tai Chi, a picture of the Buddhist deity Tara, and other participants brought along symbols that were important to them. A rich experience for another occasion would be a retreat day based around listening to explanations of these symbols. On this occasion they were acknowledged, but not explored.

Feedback received from participants was overwhelmingly very affirming. Comments included:

> 'On Friday I said ours were all different paths to the same Divine. By Sunday I could see our paths are not so different after all.'

> 'Wonderfully deep, and wonderful attunement to each other.'

> 'The weekend offered me a taste of the meditation practices of seven faith paths. What gave it richness and power for me was the sharing of deeply felt personal experience of each faith.'

For me the whole process of being moved to pick up the idea, develop it, involve others and bring it to fruition was a prayer experience. The participants' responses confirmed my sense of the convergence of paths that is there to be recognised when people are willing to explore each other's symbol and metaphor systems, because that is ultimately what each faith tradition is. All language about the Divine is metaphor. I was dancing with the Spirit, we all were. And celebrating the deep truth, the larger reality that All is indeed One.

Prayer Now
So the prayer life now of this no-longer-young church leader includes mindfulness and a great deal of silence – living alone supports this. Other time-to-time ingredients:

- the childhood prayer: 'Jesus, I love you. I love you with all my heart. Help me love you daily more and more';
- simply breathing his name, and occasionally discovering this name is already going on inside me without a conscious decision;
- just listening;
- deep awareness of Divine Mother Goddess with whom I labour to bring myself and others into wholeness;
- talking about how I feel;
- asking Sophia, Divine Wisdom for the wisdom I need;
- greeting the rising sun with a gesture of gratitude for warmth and light, or the stars, with awareness of the mystery of the cosmos, or a bird or flower;
- as a grandmother being aware of the Life that has flowed from the beginning through me, and now through these exquisite young ones; in my own spiritual direction session feeling the jolt when a guided meditation or drawing exercise hits the spot;
- exploring the world with awareness of the Loving Power that streams through us all and all that is,[5] and
- recognizing there the infinite variety of the Beloved; entering into Arvo Pärt's extraordinary tintinnabuli music *Spiegel im Spiegel* and *Für Alina*[6] which he calls white light, and which bring a deep stillness.

And very occasionally I find words that do 'do it' such as Sister Miriam Therese Winter's[7] version of the Lord's Prayer, *Our Mother who is within us...* Instead of the royal male power of the 'up there' God in the traditional version, she uses womanly imagery of One who is indwelling, who has many names, who is deeply at work within and among those who are on the life journey, gently and wisely empowering us all as individuals and as community. A very different set of metaphors from the original! When we look at the place of royalty in Aotearoa New Zealand life in the 21st century, a diminishing proportion of the community would think it very relevant. Does this mean a time might come where the old symbolism of naming God as King, Lord and Almighty could be relinquished in communal liturgy? Metaphors must evolve! And there will always be the tension between retaining beloved traditions and using words that have potent meaning now.

Two symbols have recently engaged me in prayer. Mandalas are sacred circles that indicate All is One. This is an old, old sign, currently coming into the awareness of many Christians. The other is a Möbius strip, which I'd previously known simply as a mathematical oddity. Do try this at home! Take a strip of paper that is about 3cm wide and about 25-30 cm long. Give one end a 180° twist, then join the ends with tape or staple. You now have a paradoxical one-sided solid – prove this to yourself by running a finger or drawing a line along the centre of the strip: you will traverse twice the length of the original strip and arrive back where you started. It does indeed have only one side! Now focus on a short section of the strip. Hold it between index finger and thumb. Your eyes and sense of touch tell you quite clearly that the paper has two sides. But then focusing back on the larger reality of the whole construction, you have already ascertained that it has only one side. Your 'small reality' sense information (two separate sides) has proved inadequate to give you the full truth of the 'larger reality' (All is One). This gift came via the work of David Bohm, quantum physicist, who talked of the implicate order of the universe (deep, invisible) and the explicate order (obvious, discernible by senses). A tangible demonstration of the Divine Life in and through everything!

The world of sense is so limited! And so often we act and think as though our 'small reality' sense information is all there is. Faith calls us to the acceptance and knowledge of the 'larger reality,' where we are part of this amazing whole, where quite literally, no-one and nothing is ever separated from the loving energy of the Holy Presence.

Conclusion

So prayer continues to evolve. I live with the knowledge that All is One, that we are One, sometimes as an external fact, but with hopefully ongoing and increasing inner awareness to be integrated into daily life and relationships. 'I am the Way, and the Truth and the Life' (John 14:6) has infinite depths to be explored. There is always more to discover about how the particular way, life and truth of each one of us is permeated with Divine Love.

Reluctance

Recalling one of the Voice times

Long ago
there I was
on retreat reading
a not-too-fascinating holy book
then came words –
*Strip yourself of everything
and lie before me*
What? I'm imagining things!
*Strip yourself of everything
and lie before me*
What on earth's that about?
*Strip yourself of everything
and lie before me*
God doesn't do that stuff
it must be the devil
*Strip yourself of everything
and lie before me!*
Is it really You?
You must be joking
that's really what You want?
ok, have it Your way

There, I did it
and all I got was a sore neck
from the draft under the door
now back to the book

Later at Church's Evening Prayer
the question put
with red gold fallen leaves:
*What are you not prepared
to be stripped of?*
So I heard You right!

Then came the years of it
before the time
of being re-clothed in Love

Easter Crossing 2000

Started keen
climbed labouring
heart struggle
energy gone
breath gone
he took my bag
to help me climb

Ice cold up there
thermals donned
deep fog on crater plain
a nothing space
nil visibility
past gone
future hidden
no idea what's next

Summit breakthrough
cloud gone
clarity sunshine warmth
new life new breath
pausing long to savour
the glory of seeing
forever

Then long work
of returning
to ordinary ground
changed by memory
of being close
to heaven

Only later did I see
Easter journey
Triduum
in the day we crossed
the mountain

> Remembering the first Easter weekend that I attended no church services, and realising later that the Journey had come to me.

Love and Creation

Love and Creation

Since I was a child, both in England and New Zealand, I have felt a strong connection to the natural world. In England, it was to the wild flowers whose names my mother taught me on our walks, the butterflies, tadpoles in jam-jars, the library books with tales of our wild creatures, badgers, otters, hares and more. Walks along our canal, with its fish and bird life. Her 1920s *Children's Encyclopaedia* was my first schooling, with beautiful illustrations of creatures I knew, and of those I wouldn't meet: a picture of Mary Anning finding the first ichthyosaur fossil in the Devon cliff. Then too I first heard the word 'pollution' – a bloated dead frog in a small chemical-laced patch of the canal, near a factory.

We moved to New Zealand in 1952 when I was nine. Yatton Park in Tauranga was for me a bridge between the familiar and the new. It is still a must-visit place when I'm in the area. Nearly 70 years later, I am in love with the bush of Aotearoa New Zealand. Along with the many people of many spiritual understandings, I sense the power, the depth, the energy, the peace of these holy places. They are very sacred taonga. Recent reading of *The Secret Life of Trees* (Peter Wohlleben) has taught me that trees too have consciousness, relationship, communication. I sense a welcome from the ones that know me best in Wellington's Wilton Bush. Yatton Park's Waimapu river where I learned to swim is now a sad muddy stream. Hopefully the efforts to clean up our waterways will improve its health.

From the 3-millimetre caterpillar that visited this week and the other local loves of my Earth surroundings, to the Cosmic: I'm also in love with the unbelievable glories and complexities of the universe beyond our planet. I discovered NASA's Astronomical Picture of the Day website,[46] and while the details of the explanations are mostly over my head (sorry!), the awe the images engender is a worshipful experience. And awe at the human capacity to produce a trace of a galaxy a mind-bending 60 million light years away.

Yatton Park

My first connection with nature in Aotearoa New Zealand

I first met this magical place when my family moved to Greerton in 1953. I soon made friends with the other children in the neighbourhood and they showed me what they knew simply as The Bush. It was wild in those days, completely overgrown between the huge wonderful trees. The sawmill next door was still operating, and on an adjacent side a paddock lay between it and the then end of Fraser Street. There was a steep path down the bank to the Waimapu River and local families, including mine, enjoyed a good swimming hole. It is where I first learned to swim.

Once over the cattle-stop we were in another world. We played all sorts of games there – hide-and-seek, as well as pretend explorations. In season there were things we knew we could eat – pears and walnuts from old trees, whin berries and blackberries from the tangled briars and tiny wild strawberries. Gradually I learned that there had once been a beautiful house there that had burnt down about 50 years previously. And I realised we were playing in a forsaken garden that had been carefully planned and tended – the avenue of oaks, the double curve of hydrangeas which must have bordered a path, the sheer variety of old trees.

I enjoyed the place with a variety of friends as company. But my favourite times were being there alone. I marvel now that my mother allowed me to go off there on my own for hours at a time, the only stipulation being that I did not go down to the river. I had a special little house under one of the aged hydrangeas that provided shelter and a hiding-place over a mossy floor. I communed there with the insects, the plants, whatever was happening beyond my leafy screen and with the spirit of the place. And there was a grassy glade by a soaring tree where I lay to watch the river meandering below and the clouds above. I wondered about the unknown people who had lived there long before and imagined them loving the place as much as I did. They had come, like me, from England for a new life. They had brought lots of seeds and familiar plants with them which had flourished in the new land. Would I too be able to transplant successfully and put down roots here? This was my sanctuary through some confusing times.

A few years later, my family moved south and trips north were rare. The Bush still had a powerful hold on my imagination. Thirty or so years on, I wove a short story for a writing course around those memories. It recorded my grief and dismay on my first visit back to Yatton Park in many years to find the place cleared, tamed and civilised. That reaction began at the ornamental gates and carefully designed open area, including the artificial waterfall. The cattle-stop gateway to magic had gone. Worse was to come – many of the special old trees had gone, all the undergrowth, all the hiding places, all the hydrangeas and almost all the self-seeded natives that had mingled with the immigrants' carefully planted garden. The path in the top area went right round, clearly visible from one side to the other. At least, in reality – as in my story – I was thankful that this had not been concreted.

Some of my favourite trees were still there, including the soaring Norfolk pine and the huge Queensland kauri. And eventually I was able to reflect that the changes Yatton Park had seen had some parallels to my life. It had been planted and carefully nurtured, then had the freedom to develop in its own wild way, before being simplified, clarified and made available for more people to access. The past needed to be let go!

More recently, I have appreciated the Tauranga City Council's information panels. The first private English owner of the land was John Chadwick, after whom Greerton's main street is named, and who initiated the move for a school there. He built the original homestead and called the property Yatton, probably after his native village in England. With his family he did much of the tree planting. The site of his house seems to have been where the sawmill stood later. By 1872 he and his son owned much of what is now prime Tauranga real-estate, between 18th Avenue, Cameron Road, Church Street and the Waimapu estuary. The river was then deep enough to allow small steamers access to the little wharf down the high bank. Were the wharf remnants still there when I learned to swim? Maybe!

It was interesting to discover that our street was named after Lucy Mansel, the next owner. She was an enterprising single woman who emigrated to New Zealand from England with her six nephews. They helped run the farm she'd bought. She further developed Yatton's garden and enlarged the original four room house to a large complex which became a busy social centre for the area. Lucy died in 1916. She would have been heartbroken had she seen it all destroyed by fire in 1918, the year a nephew sold it.

The following year, John Boyd, a timber miller from Taranaki bought 24 acres including the homestead site. He felled and milled the avenue of pines leading up to the house he built, and other pine trees round the property. It remained in his family until official interest began in 1953 in turning some of it into a public space. The Department of Lands bought 17½ acres. Tauranga City Council took over in 1963 and cleared and developed the park in the 1970s.

So much for the European tenure of the land. To my shame now, neither as a child nor as an adult had I ever wondered about its earlier history. When and how did it pass from Māori to Pākehā ownership? And what of the previous centuries? Again, the Council information panels and websites were enlightening and opened a whole new perspective on 'my' park. However, recorded history is silent on one crucial episode of the original transfer process from one race to the other.

For Tangata Whenua, it has always been known as one of the most important sites within Tauranga, second only to Mauao (Mount Maunganui). There was a wānanga (school) there that focused its teachings on celestial knowledge. It was set up after the arrival in Tauranga of *Tākitimu*, one of the original Māori migratory canoes. In other words, as narrated by the panels, it was a training school for tohunga, a wāhi tapu, a very sacred place.

My hair stood on end when I first read this information. No wonder I had been able to feel the spirit of the place so powerfully as a child. Just as European cathedrals have a tangible special atmosphere from being age-old sacred centres so, in my experience, does Yatton Park. It was, and I believe is still, a sacred place.

Then there is a loud gap in its history, until soon after the battles of Gate Pa and Te Ranga (1864), when the area was gifted as a reward to Hamiora Tu, one of the Māori who had assisted British troops. But who did the gifting? And how was it theirs to gift? Presumably a confiscation. Hamiora Tu soon sold it on to Chadwick. In these more enlightened days, there is a City Council care plan for the park in consultation with local iwi.

And so my relationship with the magic place of my childhood goes on, enlarged by those who have written its history, and those who, despite my mid-life grief at the drastic change, have made a beautiful green oasis with a well-recorded whakapapa, to be treasured by future generations.

Breath

In the bush
I hongi with the trees
I and my ancestors
greet you and your ancestors
we share the Sacred Breath

Wilton Bush

One day
in aeons past
a cell drank sunlight
and began the greening
that opened the path
for our becoming
In time
with breaths exchanged
there came
this symphony of greens
Celebrate Life!

Kākariki

Just

    round

        this corner

            you may find

      two red-haloed

   green angels

fossicking

amongst the leaves

murmuring gently

to each other.

You'll watch

entranced

until they

   spread

      green wings

         and disappear.

Osmosis

Walking skinless
alive with
air
water
leaves
birds
and their song
is immersion
in the Love

Morning Praise

Early on Kaukau
my mountain
I marvel at Indra's jewelled net
a spider mesh shimmering
with dew and sun
and from one angle
rainbows
singing All is One
A thousand spiders more
had spun the story
All is One!
I join the song

Labyrinth

has
but one path to the centre
here is the centre
the place to pause
the womb-tomb
the still place
to be with self
and breathe
as part of trees
as part of birds
to know All is One

The Bush

How in all the years
of walking past
did I not see you all afire with God?
Today you stopped me in my tracks
orange berries glowed like lamps
cream clusters of tiny bells
tinkled in the wind
leaves pulsed and shone
with holy energy
I worshipped

In Spring

I smell the warmth of strengthening sun
and greening world
watch grey warbler's crystal song float
through the leaves
stroke blue silk sky beyond pink
magnolia birds
taste brown bristle koru curls springing
from their centre
and hear the melt of butter on asparagus

Bee

She blundered in the open door
with two brown bags
of family provisions
I didn't see so couldn't
shepherd her towards home
with glass and paper
she died by the window
I found furry brown body
still-glistening wings
and grieved for her
and all her hard work.

Learning

As happened other springs
a tui chick perched
on the tree outside my window
to find its voice
feathers fluffed
beak agape
a shudder
A paroxysm of effort
a retching
nothing
Another fluff and shudder
a squeak
a croak
take a breath
and finally, a golden gurgle
real tui bell note
It's laugh-out-loud funny
except that would scare
the baby
away
Practice and persistence
the key
for us all!

Breakfast meditation

Fingers on brown furze
emerald mandala gleam
white centre
black specked rosette
sweet spoonful
then the crunch
of teeth on seeds

Higher tide

Dunes
tree-bone ossuary
sliver of beach
full tide surely on the turn
I walk the liminal path
skirting stripped smooth skeletons
comforting new floaters
ripped from recent soil
startled supine on the sand
still with roots and bark
pared-down beauty
driftwood sea-birds sharks
twining kelp gold on trunk
black seaweed beads on branch
interactive walk
evading playful waves

But then they rush
and claw the dunes
in menace past the play
I'm captured trapped
wet-footed
scrambling on the bones
and feel instead the fear
of land devoured by sea

> Tasting the reality of climate change.

Down South

> Getting to know a previously unvisited part of my country. A 2013 expedition.

Exploring a hitherto unvisited corner of one's own country is always enlightening and enjoyable. And so it was when a friend and I explored Stewart Island and the southeast corner of the South Island. The trip was planned well in advance and bookings made for travel and accommodation.

A late afternoon direct flight from Wellington to Invercargill got us to the first stop, with, during the flight, wonderful views of the Southern Alps and braided rivers illuminated like neon signs by the low sun. A shuttle dropped us at Tuatara Backpackers for our comfortable room plus ensuite. The pre-booked 8.30am ferry journey to Stewart Island the next day included a bus pick-up and delivery to the ferry terminal in Bluff. Despite ominous tales of the turbulence of Foveaux Strait, we enjoyed the hour-long crossing on a comparatively calm sea. February and the unusual summer weather facilitated this. The seasons of equinoctial gales are quite different!

We were met on arrival in Oban by our host Andy, of Jo and Andy's B & B, and taken to their fascinating home. Built in the 1880s, full of books and curios, homely and welcoming, it proved a great base for our three nights on the Island. The first highlight was a bus tour of the sealed road area of the island, when we were given insights into the functioning of their community, and the story of Rakiura, the Kāi Tahu name for the island. We learned that Rakiura is the anchor stone for Maui's waka from which he fished up the North Island. Links of a gigantic chain symbolising the legend 'come ashore' there, corresponding with those of the 'other end' on the Bluff coastline. And we needed a mental shift to absorb the substitution of the Southern Māori 'k' for the familiar northern 'ng.'

The visit to predator-free Ulva Island was another highlight, such rich bird-life, including a Stewart Island robin who appeared at our feet and stamped a tiny foot to encourage food to come to the surface. And yes, the bellbirds, kererū, tui, kāka and a weka. Then the magical night-time expedition to visit kiwi on a remote point of the main island. Torches, warm gear and the ability to keep quiet were all necessary as we processed silently on the easy track through the bush in single file. We paused and extinguished torches on request, and there two metres away was a large brown female kiwi fossicking in the leaf litter. We watched her a while, then gently moved on. Another further along – then two more when we reached the far beach. They like sand-hoppers for supper. What a thrill!

Culinary highlights were oyster soup at the Visitor Centre, a variety of crepes for several meals at the Crêperie, and the blue cod and chips from the hotel – takeaways half the price of eat-in. Also of interest round the town were the museum, artist workshops, the church on the hill, an assortment of easy bush and coastal walks and the DOC centre with an interesting collection of DVDs for watching in less pleasant weather.

Back in Bluff, the bus from the ferry obligingly dropped us to the rental car depot in Invercargill, where we collected our vehicle. It got us smoothly over to Kāka Point in the Catlins, by way of a stop in Gore to visit the celebrated Art Gallery. The Hotere paintings fascinated, and the Money collection of artefacts. For another three days, based at lovely Rata Cottage, we explored some of the fascinating attractions of this area. At Roaring Bay, we watched from the hide as hoiho (yellow-eyed penguins) swam in, and walked up the beach to feed their chicks, already as big as them, their evening meal of pre-digested fish. We visited the lighthouses at Nugget and Waipapa Points, the latter the site of the deadliest shipwreck in our history – 131 lives lost when the *Tararua* foundered in 1881, and its poignant cemetery just up the road.

There are the gorgeous waterfalls – Matai, McLean's and Purakaunui, all exquisite, with beautiful shortish and easy bush walks to get to them. And the awesome Cathedral Caves, down a kilometre-long track and only accessible for an hour either side of low tide, so careful planning is needed. Then Curio Bay, which deserves a chapter or book of its own. A space age viewing platform and steps provide an easy descent to the remnants of a forest that met with an overwhelming disaster 180 or so million years ago. Its stumps, now petrified, cover a significant area, challenging the mind to stretch time-wise. Alongside is a rocky cleft, sides covered with golden growing kelp. As each wave rushes in then out, the kelp dances and squirms like demented linguini, first in one direction, then the other. The fossilised forest can only be accessed a couple of hours either side of low tide.

Ōwaka is the central town for the area. It boasts two good cafés, a great new museum, the cottage industry Catlins Soap Factory and a bizarrely interesting Teapot Land, an outdoor display of hundreds of them. Also, petrol. We discovered the next advertised pump some kilometres south does not do Sundays, so had to head on to Fortrose for a refill.

Heading north, we visited the albatross colony on the Otago Peninsula. A second visit on a windier day to watch from the car-park gave more glimpses of the majestic birds than we'd had on our official visit. Moeraki boulders give another glimpse of the ancient processes that have shaped Aotearoa New Zealand. As does the collection of fossils at the Vanished World Centre in Duntroon in the Waitaki Valley which has become a centre for geological education. Many fascinating items, including a scary 80 cm jawbone of an extinct saw-tooth dolphin from the 25 million years ago when the area, now well inland, was under the ocean.

Lake Tekapō has a multitude of attractions, but we were there to visit the observatory at Mount John. As star-viewing is necessarily weather dependent, booking on the day is recommended. We were in luck – a clear evening for the twilight tour, the time of which varies through the year. A short minibus ride took us from the town agency to the summit of the hill outside the town. It is 'the biggest and best dark-sky reserve in the world', recognised in 2012 by UNESCO. And then two hours of awe! The sun disappeared in the west, the moon rose full and yellow in the east. Stars became visible.

Through some of their telescopes we saw Jupiter and its moons, breathtakingly beautiful constellations called Jewel Box and Wishing Well, Matariki, and most stretchingly of all a fuzzy patch of stars outside our solar system, some 1600 light years away, and 10 to12 billion years old... And our own moon, huge, pitted, almost touchable.

Back in the here and almost-now, the new Te Ana Centre in Timaru is well worth a visit. It preserves and traces the history of the many examples of Māori rock art locally and nationally. It is another place for revering the past. Then the very here-and-now of a morning at the Winton-Geraldine A & P Show, a great glimpse of rural New Zealand and the people and animals who make it tick. Dog trials, goats, sheep, cattle, alpacas, donkeys, horses – and a competition for women riding side-saddle! And the children's wonderful critters made from vegetables. We were well grounded again after the adventures in time and space.

Two happy visits to friends and relations got us back to Christchurch and the flight home. An enriching two weeks well spent making the acquaintance of some of the fascinating places Down South.

The Stardust Revolution: The New Story of Our Origin in the Stars

A review from a 2014 read – and so much more has been discovered since then. [47]

This book broadened my horizons – or more accurately blew them to smithereens! A literal horizon is the boundary line between earth and the heavens, and this book is the story of the dismantling of that boundary by astronomer-scientists of the last half century or so. That complex science can be an enthralling read to someone who only did it to fourth-form level is an astonishing feat of narration. Berkowitz calls his story extreme genealogy: the primary question is 'where did we come from?'

I was attracted by the subtitle: The New Story of Our Origins in the Stars. When one comes from a scriptural/theological perspective, such a theme has to be relevant. Most 21st century Christians, in Aotearoa New Zealand anyway, have no trouble integrating evolution as propounded by Darwin into their theology, or the Big Bang that preceded that theory by a few billion years. The same events or processes can be variously described by poems (Genesis) or newspaper reports (basic science) or scientific treatises. So I'd been thinking of Earth as a hunk of rock, where life mysteriously began in a soup and is evolving with Divine guidance.

But Jacob Berkowitz and his gallery of star-gazing scientists have caused another big bang in my awareness. He traces the discoveries that in their birthings and dyings, the stars manufacture the basic chemical elements of which absolutely everything is made. That the universe is expanding. (I looked in vain for Kiwi cosmologist Beatrice Tinsley who proved this.) That the space between the stars is filled with cosmic dust. That in this cosmic dust is water, all our earthly elements and organic traces. That life was probably seeded onto primeval earth by this dust. That we are thus literally made of this stardust. That other solar systems have planets, and the hunt is on for one or more in their 'Goldilocks' (not too hot, not too cold) zones for an earth-like one where life could be possible. That there are now speciality disciplines of astrophysics, astrochemistry, astrobiology and astrogeology.

So what does all this mean in theological terms? God gets a respectful mention or two along the way. One scientist is quoted as saying if God didn't do it like that, He (sic) missed a good bet. But for me the profound moment comes when the author asks a scientist if he could define Life. The reply: 'Life is love.' The impulse to connect and combine is 'built into' the components of atoms, and thereby into everything else, including us. All the Christian injunctions to love God and neighbour are to steer us into living in harmony with this cosmic process. All in all, this is an incredibly more awesome Creation story than Adam and Eve! Nonetheless it is fascinating that the order of creation in Genesis as described 5,000 plus years ago is pretty much the sequence in which science describes evolution today.

But then what? How does this new knowledge get incorporated into the on-going Christian story? How does it modify or affirm the language that is traditionally used to transmit this story? How can Cosmos be articulated in our liturgies when they have been traditionally worded around the ancient three-tier universe's geography of heaven, earth and hell? If the life of Jesus is pivotal to the human story, he is an evolutionary turning point. He revealed our essential one-ness with each other and with God as a counter to inter-tribal and inter-personal struggles over difference. Now science is providing the hard-wiring for all that – we humans are all one with each other and with all that is on Planet Earth and in the Cosmos.

Thank you to the patient, methodical men and women, past and present, who study stars. And thank you to Jacob Berkowitz for one of the most exciting bits of learning I've had for years! It has left me, two readings later, with a high of cosmic proportions! And an even greater awe for my God as both Transcendent and as all-permeating Life-Force, as the Power of Love.

Love and Community

Love and Community

Community is about being connected. This section looks at my relationships with the human world around me. My primary community is my family: my six wonderful home-grown offspring and my foster daughter, their life-partners, and their children, all 21 of them. Then there is my ex-daughter-in-law, dear friend, superb rearer of two grandchildren and her new in-law family. All much loved! But not written about.

The writings in this section begin with a one-to-one relationship. As already mentioned, spiritual direction has been a crucial thread of my journey. This is one of the treasures for centuries practised in the Catholic Church for priests and Religious. In the 1980s in Aotearoa New Zealand, two Presbyterian ministers asked to be trained in the art. Since then, an interdenominational programme has developed to make the training available to lay people, and a national association with its code of ethics. I did this training myself in 1990. Spiritual Growth Ministries also has a yearly programme offering retreats and workshops in all parts of the country, and there is *Refresh,* New Zealand Journal of Contemplative Spirituality.

Then a friendship story. All my friends are precious companions and nurturing these relationships is important. The regular connectings and the now-and-then ones. Last December I lunched with four women from my last year at school at St Mary's, Wellington. We marvelled that it was exactly 60 years since we had left school together. With some there has been a close connection right through, with others more sporadic. The following week was a lunch with four others with whom I'd begun at Tauranga College in 1955. Both groups have had such varied lives, and we value our yearly or so meet-up. In both, we note who is no longer with us, and gratefully celebrate our own ongoing lives. Other friends with significant disabilities are a constant inspiration. I come from being with them humbled and taught about courage, resilience and depth.

My suburban neighbourhood is another community where there are good connections, communication and caring. Brilliant in the time of the Covid-19 virus lock-down. And there is my parish, St Andrew's on The Terrace. More of those later.

As my understanding of other faith traditions has grown, some beautiful personal relationships have developed where we can celebrate diversity by deep sharing of our faiths and practices.

Spiritual Direction

When I'm receiving –
I go where I can be me
wholly me
holy ground
years-long golden thread
with wiser ones
where moments of awareness
can be recalled explored enriched
where wisdom from
the Beyond-Within
can throw more light
on the path behind
the now
the path ahead
You are in and through it all

When I'm offering –
there's the long slow listen
once You called me 'lodestone'
then I didn't understand
but now can see the process
of participating in the re-setting
of each one's compass
as being held
wholly and holy in Your hands
sharing the 'not knowing'
darkness and light
pain dreams intuitions growth ecstasy
with the sure knowing
that You respond
to searching souls
and through all that
the passed-on wisdom –
you can take people no deeper
than you've gone yourself

A True Story

> The family asked for their real names to be used. It was such a privilege to be a part of this story! It was written for her grandchildren.

Once upon a time, not so many decades ago, a good woman had a baby boy. Because she loved him and didn't believe she could look after him as well as he deserved, she entrusted him to another father and mother who brought him up and helped him grow into a good man. A while later, the same thing happened again and another baby boy was entrusted to another father and mother, and he too was helped to grow into a good man.

The good woman grieved for her babies and was not proud of being unable to look after them. As she got older, she kept it a secret from the people she knew. A long time later her church community had some special meetings where they talked to each other about God and real things that had happened in their lives. For the first time she heard two other women talking about grieving for their babies whom they had had to entrust to others. Still she said nothing. But later she did tell someone about her babies. And later again she asked that woman to look after her when she might not be able to look after herself.

About that time, Charlie, the younger of the two boys who were now men, discovered who his birth-mother was and came halfway round the world for a special visit with his beautiful wife and little girl. Later he came back to visit again, this time with Liz, the lovely mum who had brought him up. She was so grateful to his birth mum for allowing her to be his mother too. When they had gone back, Bridget, for that was her name, sighed and wished she could go across another sea to find her older son, James. Her friends talked about it, but decided she really wasn't well enough for a trip like that and anyway, where would they start looking? One found a very old address and they decided to write a letter to James and hope it might reach him. The letter said that if he wanted to get in touch with his birth mum, it would be good to do that as she was getting frailer. And it asked if he knew he had a half-brother. There was no reply and the friends thought, 'Well, we tried.'

Weeks and weeks later, one friend found a message from James on her answerphone. She was puzzled for a moment: James who? Then realised – this was the reply to the letter! But how could she contact him in Australia? Then he rang again, and what a surprise! – he and his family had been back living in New Zealand for a long time. The letter had been on a very long journey there and back and had eventually reached him. When he got it, he'd jumped on a plane and had arrived at Wellington Airport. The friend jumped into her car, went to meet him there and they talked for a long time, and were both happy with what they discovered. James asked, 'Can I see her tomorrow?' The friend said she'd do her best, and later got in touch with the others to arrange a ride for him.

Next morning, she went to see Bridget, and tried to be very gentle.

'Do you remember you said you'd really like to see James?' 'Mmm', said Bridget a bit sadly.

'Well, we wrote a letter to his old address in Australia.' 'Mmm, that was nice of you.'

'But he and his family came back to New Zealand a long time ago.' 'Oh?' – interested now!

'Now he's just got the letter, and he's come to Wellington.' 'Really?!' – cautious delight!

'He'd like to see you – can he come this morning?' Tears, 'It's a miracle!' and 'Yes, yes!' So the other friend brought James to Bridget, and it was an amazing moment of reunion for them, and for the friends.

James discovered he had a new extra family with lots of aunties and uncles and cousins, and in a while brought his beautiful wife and children to meet Bridget and the rest of the family. The idea of a brother he'd never known about still seemed quite strange, though. He visited Bridget a few times and got to know her as a good, kind, gentle woman. It was still a long journey from his home, so it couldn't be very often.

A few years passed, and one day Bridget got very sick. That weekend, James and Sandra came down to see her. She was very pleased to see them, then they went home. When they'd heard how sick she was, Charlie and Fay decided they too would travel from England to see her again the next weekend. When James and Sandra heard this was happening, they decided it would be the right moment to meet his brother, so they came back to Wellington again. They all met for the first time, and it made them very happy! The next morning, they went to see Bridget together, and for the first and only time she had her two boys with her at the same time. Her life was complete – she had seen them again, and seen them together as her two sons, and as brothers to each other, and as husbands to two other good women and fathers to her grandchildren. Then they all went back to their homes.

The very next weekend she got even sicker and seemed likely to die soon. When he heard this, James jumped in his car and all night drove the very, very long way to be with her. He arrived and held her hand, the nurses were looking after her too, and within a little while she died. Soon he found a bed to have a sleep, then got back in his car and drove all the way home. Charlie and Fay were very sad too, but so glad they had been for their visit, had seen Bridget, and had met James and Sandra and become family with them. Now they could talk to each other.

For the fourth time in four weeks, James came to Wellington, this time with Sandra, for Bridget's funeral. He talked to everyone there about his life and getting to know Bridget and her family. Sandra read the beautiful letter from Charlie and Fay. James shared some powerful words he had discovered in his heart that summed up the whole enormous experience:

In the beginning, it was Mum, me and the nurses.

In the end, it was Mum, me and the nurses.

James and Charlie and Sandra and Fay made Bridget very happy. She died as a loved and fulfilled mother, with all threads of her life at last connected into a beautiful pattern.

Rātana

> Visiting the home of a Māori form of Christianity

Waitangi Day 2012 seemed a fitting occasion to join a friend who was going to visit Rātana, the headquarters of the Rātana Church near Whanganui. We could perhaps attend any celebrations being held there. When we arrived, however, on a warm summery day, the streets of the small settlement (population about 400) were deserted – our cars were the only vehicles in view. Except that is, for the local fire-engine stopped by the side of the road, with its fully-equipped fireman who leapt into the middle of the road with his STOP sign as the engine reversed into its station. So we stopped. And chatted to the fireman, and then his mates too. They were Thomas, Dave and Mick, locals and volunteers who had been out on a training exercise. They were curious about why we were there, and the conversation quickly turned to spirituality. We really did want to understand more about their faith and founder. Could anyone tell us more about that? 'We'll get Harry,' they said. Harry Docherty (a great-grandson of Rātana, we learned later) duly arrived and was very willing to tell a couple of respectfully curious pākehā some of what he knew.

So we walked the block back to the Temple, gleaming white behind its immaculate white wall, and along the way heard more about the founder himself. And that their large-scale celebrations on 25 January to mark Ratana's birthday meant that Waitangi Day was not formally celebrated in the village. January is their major occasion when 1000 plus visitors arrive and the media scrutinise the contributions of politicians who come along.

Tahupotiki Wiremu Ratana was a farmer who on 8 November 1918, had a vision of Archangel Gabriel. He was told he had been empowered to heal and preach the gospel and was to be known as Te Mangai (the Mouthpiece of God), and his followers were to be known as Mōrehu (The Remnant). His mission was to unite his people and lead them from traditionally understood evil spirits, tohunga-ism, black magic and jealousy, to the One True God. His tomb in the grounds of the temple depicts in marble the essence of his mission: he held in his right hand the Holy Bible and in his left Te Titiriti o Waitangi. In that alone, from the vantage point of 2012, he can be recognised as prophetic.

He preached and healed in the Way of the Son, and the ranks of his followers grew. Pākehā were also healed, and many of these events around the country were documented.

A village had sprung up round his farm. A world tour with a leadership group in 1924 led to a strong connection with Bishop Juji Nakada in Japan who hosted Rātana and his party. A centre for worship was planned for the Rātana people.

The temple, Te Temepara Tapu O Ihoa, was publicly blessed on 25 January 1928, Ratana's 55th birthday. Bishop Nakada attended and had supplied blue and purple stained glass for the windows.

Its exterior architecture shows influences from European, Japanese and Spanish Mission styles he had seen during his extensive travels. It features two Romanesque bell towers. He called them Arepa and Ōmeka (Alpha and Omega). Two of his sons also bore these names. 'They represented the two phases of Rātana's ministry: Ture Wairua or spiritual works, where he was engaged in lifting curses, healing, challenging the old gods and teaching from the Bible; and the Ture Tangata or physical works, where he was increasingly concerned with the welfare of the people, calling Māori tribes to unify and collecting signatures for a petition to Parliament to revive the Treaty of Waitangi.' (Historic Places Trust)

The interior of the temple features a traditional Methodist format: at the front are the table and tiered seats for the apostles, choir and brass band. It can seat up to 1000. As a visual teaching to his then largely illiterate followers, he planned the colour-coded theological diagram on the wall above featuring Matua (The Father – blue), Tama (The Son – white), Wairua Tapu (The Holy Spirit – red), Anahera (Angels – purple) and Te Mangai (The Mouthpiece – i.e. Ratana himself – gold). Painted loops of chain in the same colours continue round the walls connecting the stars (whetū mārama) that are the main symbol of the Ratana movement. They too have colour-coded segments. They signify Māramatanga, the Kingdom of Light, which stands firm against the forces of darkness (mākutu).

The striking Glory Hallelujah archway at the temple gate was dedicated in 1935 to the memory of his sons Hamuera (Samuel), Arepa and Omeka who had all died. Its inscription reads: 'Te Arepa the beginning, Te Omeka the end, Hamuera the last full stop. Therefore, this treasured memorial now stands revealed, from now on the Spirit will do its work and you shall know its fruits.'

After Rātana's death on 18 September 1939, some of the buildings at Ratana, including the temple, were deteriorating. From the 1940s Ratana's sister, Puhi o Aotea, and subsequently his daughter Maata 'Te Reo' Hura led various stages of restoration work.

From the temple, Harry took us the couple of blocks, past well-tended homes, to the marae. Along the way we saw the only obvious building of Māori design bearing the sign Whare Māori. To our query he replied that that was where a lot of curses were kept locked up. The marae Manuao is a large green European-style building opened in 1938, whose most notable feature from outside is the array of nine sea going vessels along its frontage. There are the seven waka of the Great Fleet, *Tākitimu, Te Arawa, Aotea, Tainui, Kurahaupō, Mātaatua* and *Tokomaru*. And at the end of the row, in a moving gesture of inclusion, there too are the *Heemskirck*, Abel Tasman's ship, and Cook's *Endeavour*. Nearby is the farmhouse on whose veranda Rātana had his vision.

Then Harry left us to ponder what we'd seen and heard. We'd had a glimpse into the life, faith, worship and history of a village like no other, where virtually all the inhabitants belong to the same faith. Ratana had an early connection with the Methodist Church, which in 2011 formally chose to share governance equally between Taha Māori and Tauiwi groupings, as an outcome of taking seriously its obligations under Te Tiriti. He was, from his heavenly home, undoubtedly delighted and fulfilled. And his 50,000 present-day followers will likewise have been encouraged with some of the developments of their founder's key teaching, in the right hand the Holy Bible and in the left Te Titiriti o Waitangi, as more of the Christian Churches in Aotearoa acknowledge partnership obligations.

Mahboba's Promise

Connecting with Islam.[48]

On 22 February 2011, I made a promise. A promise to write about a woman whose life-work is the keeping of a promise. The Christchurch earthquake and other things intervened, but later came the time to keep the promise.

We were at an early evening meeting of the Pan Pacific and South East Asia Women's Association in suburban Wellington to listen to Mahboba Rawi, an Afghan Australian, talking about her work for the widows and children of Afghanistan. We still had not understood the magnitude of the events unfolding in Christchurch. Our focus was on this woman who was travelling to enlist support for the victims of war in her homeland.

Very occasionally during life one meets a person through whom the light of God shines brightly. Mahboba is such a person. Radiant, strong, brown eyes lit from within, a beautiful blue scarf draped as head-covering, a devout Muslim and a loyal and appreciative Australian of 26 years standing.

She told us her life story. Born to a comfortably off family of nine children in Kabul, she was the one with whom her father, unusually, chose to share his wisdom and knowledge as well as with her brothers. When she started secondary school, she had ambitions to study at university and become a doctor – possible then! As a young teenager she experienced the Russian invasion of 1979, and when the older student who had initiated political protest and resistance by students was arrested, Mahboba stepped up as the next leader. She and others were soon rounded up and were loaded into a bus to be taken to an unknown destination. She managed to escape, hid from pursuing soldiers in a carpet shop, was hidden by relatives for weeks while the family organised her escape with her uncle through the mountains to the freedom of Pakistan.

After her journey across the Khyber Pass, she was fortunate to have relations to stay with at the refugee camp. But she was very aware of the uneven distribution of aid to refugees in camps. She dreamed of being in charge of getting aid to those who most needed it. She and a brother eventually got to India, where she married an Afghan man already resettled in Australia and joined him there in 1984. She had their two children and began working to help other Afghan women settle into their new home and culture with education programmes and community initiatives. Further tragedy hit when their son drowned in an accident. She had another son, however her marriage eventually foundered. From the depths of pain, she began a deep spiritual journey and prayed to God to find a new purpose in life. That purpose came when a doctor in the Pakistani refugee camps asked for help to save children from starving. Mahboba started collecting funds, first to feed the children and then to provide education for camp children. In 2001, she started helping children in Afghanistan with the help of her uncle who travelled to Kabul and found his old house still standing. The ongoing and at times accelerating killing had left countless widows and their children with no means of support.

On her first visit back to her homeland in 2002, she was shocked to see children as young as five trying desperately to sell trivia like chewing gum and plastic bags in the streets to earn the family some food. She went home with one child and spoke with the mother. 'I will pay you more than she has been earning if you can let her go to school.' A promise! It was kept. And with the help of her equally remarkable uncle and generous donors in Australia and elsewhere, she has been able to keep that promise and open refuges that currently support 500 widows and their children in Kabul and beyond. Mahboba raised funds to build Hope House where there is food, love, education, some security – and hope of a sustainable future with employment education for the women.

Her energetic fund-raising activities long since grew beyond her garage in Sydney. A formal organisation was set up and became known as Mahboba's Promise Inc. A documentary on her work was shown on Australian television and gained much support. During one visit to Afghanistan she met a man who wished to marry her because he had seen the documentary. Not at all her choice, but after prayer and laying down some ground rules, she accepted. He would have to respect her work, her independence, her travel. Not the image of a Muslim marriage that Westerners usually have! So he too is now in Australia, and her main support. Her first husband had insisted that she not wear a head-covering in their new country in an effort to fit in. For many years she concurred. But eventually she chose to resume the custom of covering her hair as a sign of her dedication to God's call.

We listened fascinated to this extraordinary story – mostly white Kiwi women, and a dozen or so Muslim women. We saw sections of the video – widows in incongruously pretty blue burqas sitting begging in the squalid pot-holed streets of Kabul, children selling shoelaces, Hope House where there were smiles and gratitude from the mums and their children for being given another chance at a human life. Wars are always a catastrophe for the young. They grow up scarred, and if nothing changes, the boys are likely to become yet another generation of warriors. For those cared for by Mahboba's Promise, there is hope for future peace.

God and God's work are central to Mahboba's life. She cares passionately what happens to the women and children of her tortured homeland. She works to provide them with the basics – and hope. And she appreciates any assistance in support of her work.

Tibetan Journeys

> A study tour that became a pilgrimage with a mission.

Tibet is a land of mystery, mountains and paradox which I visited for a week in September 2011. A week is a woefully inadequate time to understand in any depth the realities of people and place, particularly when the situation is so complex. So this is simply a Kiwi traveller's tale, with observations filled out a little by reading and reflection.

There was much to ponder before we went on the tour, and even more on our return. So many differing perspectives and stories! There is the highest respect here and round the world for His Holiness the Dalai Lama. His goodness, compassion and unwavering stand on non-violence have earned this from people of all faiths and none and have undoubtedly increased the focus on his Tibetan form of Buddhism. While Buddhism is in many aspects quite different from Christianity, many scholars and mystics like the late Thomas Merton have over the last few decades engaged in dialogue and recognition of common ground.

There is too the struggle for the hearts and minds of the Tibetan people whose human rights have been systematically undermined by the Chinese occupiers. The Chinese Government believes it has a long-standing right to govern this area. It was clear that we would be visiting an occupied land, the streets of whose capital Lhasa have run with the blood of protesters as recently as 2008. There has too been large-scale immigration of Han Chinese to the point where Tibetans are now a minority in their own land, and significantly disadvantaged in multiple ways. Colonisation, as happened here and elsewhere in the 1800s.

Before leaving home, I was given a pendant with a relic of Tulku Chagdud Rinpoche, a lama who escaped from Tibet to Nepal in the 1950s, subsequently had an international teaching career and died in Brazil in 2006. 'Take him back to visit his homeland,' said my friend. It is silver. One side has a central turquoise mounted in the centre of a dorje, a symbol for compassion and strength. The other side features the universal chant – Om mani padme hum – in Tibetan script. This turned the expedition for me into something of a pilgrimage. I learned that Tulku signifies someone who is a recognised reincarnation, Chagdud was the lama who was reincarnated, and Rinpoche means teacher. And that his mastery of the mind was such that he meditated for six days after taking his last breath before finally leaving his body, an event that is hard for western minds to comprehend or begin to understand.

The depths of Buddhist teaching on mind and body goes way beyond anything familiar to western/Christian faith and practice. So I was keen to see whether we would meet any learned monks in any of the half dozen monasteries we were scheduled to visit, wondered whether the pendant might be a potent way to connect, and decided that if it became appropriate I would leave the pendant in its true home.

Our tour group had a Kiwi tour leader, a Chinese in-country guide, a kind and helpful man and member of the Chinese Communist party, and then there were the local guides who spent a few days each with us as we were in their region. The one in Tibet specifically announced he would not be discussing politics. We acclimatised for a week in Yunnan province at steadily increasing altitudes.

This included a two-night stay in Zhongdian, a 'Tibetan area' of China, which is also known as Shangri-La, after the Hilton novel based there. Some of us went to a local 'cultural show'. This turned out to be an astoundingly sophisticated sound, light and dance show based on Tibetan culture and depicting the path to enlightenment of a pilgrim. Both the technical aspects and the honouring of the culture and dharma (teaching) were obviously permitted or even encouraged by Chinese authorities, with its current policy of preserving minorities but within carefully monitored limits. We also visited a very substantial Tibetan home, with a beautiful older woman as our hostess. She was happy to have us explore her home and take photos in the large multi-purpose and colourfully decorated main room. The pendant did its first task as a communicator – such a wonderful excited smile when I showed her the prayer on its reverse and asked the local guide to tell her it had come from Tibet to New Zealand and now had returned.

From there to the Tibetan Autonomous Region proper. After a flight over snow covered mountains and an interesting u-turn descent, we landed at Lhasa Airport. Then by bus to the city on a good road, part motorway, and through another mountain or two. At last there was the city, with the red and white Potala Palace prominent on its hill top. The city itself was modern with shops and multi-storey buildings. The Chinese have poured hundreds of billions of yuan into creating an infrastructure: roading, power, sewage, transport and the Lhasa-Beijing railway we rode on later. There must have been some expectation that this would elicit gratitude and cooperation from the indigenous population. But it seems that 60 years on hearts and minds have not been won over. Somewhere along our way there was an older woman with a bag embroidered with the English words Free Tibet. And there was the man who beamed and shook hands when he was shown my pendant, then hitched up his jacket to reveal an illegal portrait of the Dalai Lama well hidden in his clothing. A moving gesture of trust.

Over the next week we visited half a dozen monasteries and temples, which had the sad effect of turning the rest of the group off Buddhism. In one a monk was sitting literally counting his money, taking a few seconds off now and then to give a blessing, thereby acquiring more. Large numbers of pilgrims crowded through, many prostrating their way in, praying before the multitudinous statues of Buddha, bodhisattvas, disciples and teachers, and leaving money at each pause point. I wondered where the real strength and consolation drawn from faith fades and other descriptions such as Marx's 'opiate of the people' become also valid.

I and others recognised that we were being shown what the Chinese authorities had decided to let us see. Perhaps some of it was a staged attempt to justify their crackdown on monastic life and reducing it to a shadow of its former power. The monks totally ignored us. Back home later I found an internet item saying they do not interact with tourists as the temples are swarming with secret police. Expecting to meet the essence of Buddhist wisdom in such places was on a par with expecting to find the essence of Christian mysticism on a visit to St Peter's in Rome. I spent a lot of time saying all religions have their dark and light sides.

Then there was the squad of about 20 Chinese soldiers lined up in the main Barkhor square near the central most revered Jokhang temple, rifles drawn, and another group marching in, whether to supplement or replace we didn't stay to see. An ominously uncomfortable experience! Here was oppression writ large. When our tour leader asked the in-country guide what that was about, 'perhaps an important visitor?' he simply replied, 'The Dalai Lama'.

Visiting the Norbulinka, the former summer palace, on a sunny morning, enjoying the beautiful gardens and many interesting buildings, seemed a world away from 10 March 1959 when it was the scene of carnage as thousands gathered to protect the Dalai Lama. He escaped disguised as a soldier and fled to India in the hope that this would avoid bloodshed. It didn't.

After three days we boarded our comfortable new bus and headed west over two mountain passes. One summit was at an altitude of 5,000 metres, comparable to the Everest base camp. The road as we climbed was a triumph of Chinese engineering, a solid highway with concrete edging, and an interesting lack of safety barriers between us and increasingly precipitous drops. It helped to know that our driver was an owner-operator of the vehicle, and we'd already experienced his skill. We were heading for Gyantse then Shigatse, Tibet's second largest city. Why a road of this quality? And who had done the actual building? Unlikely to be simply for the benefit of tourists. Other reading had revealed the Chinese interest in the many mineral riches of the Tibetan western plateau, the nuclear missiles arrayed there and the dumping of imported nuclear waste.

The scenery over the passes was stunning: gigantic snow-capped peaks, glaciers in retreat, a turquoise sacred lake, hills draped with the ubiquitous prayer flags, roadside shrines. Five major rivers of Asia have their sources in this area: the Yangtze, Yellow, Mekong, Brahmaputra and Salween. There is real concern that, compounded by the large-scale deforestation and global warming, their health is being compromised in a way that will affect millions of people throughout Asia.

We visited another private home on that leg of the journey and again were warmed by the hospitable reception. We wondered at the yak dung patties drying on walls outside, including those of the house, providing insulation as they did so. They provide good odour-free fuel in a land where trees are now pretty scarce. It was a three-generation home, the grandmother was giving kind care to a little boy of maybe five who had a significant disability and was unable to stand – but smiled anyway. Then there were younger women and their children and husbands. We'd heard of a tradition still practised in those areas where a woman is married to two or three brothers at once. It means there are more hands to work whatever land is available and children are raised by all the adults together. Our host family may not have been like this.

I asked the Chinese guide whether the Government provided any assistance for children with disabilities. Yes, it did. Does that family receive any? He didn't know whether they 'accessed' any. The local Tibetan guide's comment to another member of the group was more chilling; 'He will fall over and die sometime'.

One of our group was particularly keen to see Gyantse as his grandfather had been part of the British Younghusband incursion in 1904, and taken part in the battle where they had routed the ill-equipped Tibetans. The castle on the hill that was taken then is being restored. Gyantse looked like a border town, with a hotel that was much more comfortable than we'd been led to expect. Shigatse was in the process of becoming a modern city, but the roads were dug up, some with deep craters – permafrost apparently causes major engineering problems.

It became obvious that we were being carefully managed and monitored. Our bus had to arrive at several police checkpoints along the route at stipulated times. Do not be early. Do not be late. Do not deviate from the required route. And even more revealingly, some of us decided we'd like to visit the local nunnery in Shigatse, not far from our hotel, to see how the women's lives were being lived – we'd seen plenty of male establishments. We mentioned this to the Chinese guide. He visibly blanched, and said, 'No, you can't do that. We have no permit. If you go, they will shut my firm down.' So we didn't.

We were warmly welcomed by the women who worked in the carpet factory at Shigatse. Skilled and cheerful, they seemed genuinely happy in their work and with each other's company. Sitting cross legged on the floor for hours seemed comfortable enough, whether spinning on primitive wheels the wool brought down from the plateau by nomads, winding it into skeins, or knotting the colourful carpets. Their children were with them at work, one baby asleep on a mat on the floor by his mum. After we'd left the sounds of a cheerful communal song enhanced the impression that they were among the fortunately employed ones.

They certainly seemed more fortunate than the women we'd seen breaking stones with hand tools for road works, and those carrying rocks on small plywood back-boards at a monastery reconstruction site. One sang as she made repeated trips with what looked like a back-breaking load. We asked the local guide what she was singing. 'About how happy and fulfilling her life is,' he replied.

On the way back to Lhasa via a different route along the river, we stopped near a barren-looking hill and were told it was a sky-burial site. This is another custom that is quite alien to western minds. When people die, their bodies are carried up to one of these sites where they are ceremonially cut up and fed to vultures. In practical terms this makes sense, the ground is frozen for much of the year, and there is no timber for cremation except for very high lamas. In spiritual terms this is understood as returning the souls to the ether by courtesy of the sacred birds. I'd thought this custom might still be practised in remote areas, but it seemed to be a norm as this hill was relatively close to Lhasa. We didn't discover what the funeral customs of the Chinese majority entailed.

Another night in the capital, then an early morning departure from the newish railway station to begin our 23-hour journey to Xining in northern Tibet. Uniformed station attendants wearing white gloves saluted as the train pulled out. The Lhasa to Golmud link is the highest railway in the world, and cabins are pressurised like aircraft and have an oxygen feed. It crosses mountainous country and high plateaus rising to over 5000m. It was opened in 2006 and is a significant feat of engineering. The ride was smooth with a good dining car and comfortable four berth cabins. Majestic and formerly pristine wilderness is now bisected by this railway and festooned with power lines. Herds of yaks appeared at intervals, and infrequent clusters of dwellings. To their credit, the engineers had built occasional tunnels under the line to facilitate the movement of animals, but ecology and fauna have still been massively affected. Large sections of the line are built over permafrost and there are questions about its stability should global warming cause any significant thawing. This huge project too is not just for the benefit of tourists. It facilitates the movement of people, goods and potentially military reinforcement to and from the heart of Tibet.

And so we moved out of the Tibetan Autonomous Region of China after a week of fascinating glimpses of an ancient faith-filled culture and a modern oppressive occupation. What one can see in a week barely scratches the surface. And what, we wondered, did the 'Autonomous' signify?

The reading has continued – autobiographies of the Dalai Lama, his sister, his mother, his personal physician, with their stories of torture, human rights abuses, traumatic escapes. And the struggles to negotiate with the Chinese Government, to enlist support from countries in the West, to establish democratic processes within the large-scale Tibetan resettlement in India and Nepal, to nurture the faith, language and culture of the hundreds of thousands of refugees who have crossed the Himalayas to freedom. The women's stories are particularly interesting, giving accounts of family life, traditions and beliefs before and during the disruptions of the last sixty years.

Another perspective was offered by a Chinese doctoral student studying in USA who suffered a severe culture shock when he observed the reverence with which the Dalai Lama is regarded there. His own education had been very different – he had learned to describe this man as 'a rebellious separatist' to be despised, if not actually hated. He may also have heard the description of His Holiness as 'a wolf with the face of a man but the heart of an animal.' And he pondered the political power of education.

He protests, with some justification, that the image of Tibet as an idyllic peaceful heaven on earth before the Chinese 'liberation' is a myth. While the ordinary people may have been peace-loving and happy, the lives of many were poverty-stricken, maternal and child health was woefully inadequate, huge taxes were demanded by the Government and monasteries, and despite the Buddhist belief in compassion there was a lot of internecine violence. The history of the office of the Dalai Lama reads like a catalogue of murders, poisonings and kidnappings. Warlords were engaged in power struggles in their areas. The Dalai Lama's mother relates the widespread suspicion that her husband was poisoned. Also that when her son's regent returned from an absence, his role was not handed back as agreed and he died in prison, probably murdered. He had himself put another man in prison and had his eyes gouged out.

Tibet continues to be in the news. In the last year there have been 34 self-immolations mostly by monks and nuns while crying out for the Dalai Lama. And recently there was news of Tibetans being shot and killed because of demonstrating an on-going refusal to celebrate Chinese Year and protesting against the official cancellation of Tibetan New Year Lohar celebrations in February. The Dalai Lama last year stepped away from political leadership of his people, while retaining the spiritual role. The Tibetan communities in India have embraced democracy and integration of Western science while retaining their culture and Buddhist faith. He continues to seek the cooperation of his 'Chinese brothers and sisters' in regaining basic human rights for Tibetans including the right to live according to their beliefs. Sixty years on there is no real sign that this is a possibility. But astonishing turnarounds can happen – like glasnost and the fall of the Berlin Wall and recently in Myanmar/Burma.

And the pendant? It came home with me – we had no direct access to any monks. A scheduled visit to a Living Buddha became 'unavailable.' But it had done its work as a rapport builder with ordinary people along the way, along with my one word in Tibetan – tashi delek – which, like kia ora, has many uses in greeting and thanking. It was a fascinating privilege to visit this remote and beautiful land and to meet the friendly people who have been through so much. The Dalai Lama has said, 'Visit Tibet and bear witness.' And so I have!

Gallipoli

> A painful visit during a tour of Turkey

Where is the monument
to the women of Gallipoli?
to those who with blood sweat and tears
gave birth to those boys
those men
not for this
to those who waited and watched
from home
tending children
doing what was necessary
to keep life moving and fed
for when they'd all come back
not for this
to those women who freer to move
tended the jobs
that had been left behind
learned new skills
still daughters, sisters, fiancées
not for this

As news came, all these
on their own Calvaries

Encountering Rumi

> A joyful antidote to the horror at Gallipoli was visiting the tomb of a man of peace.[49]

The writings of Mevlana Jelaludin Rumi are finding a space in the hearts of many Christians and others in the 21st century. He was an Islamic mystic, poet, philosopher and apostle of tolerance who was born in 1207 in Persia and lived most of his life in Konya. This city was then in the Ottoman Empire and is now in the centre of modern Turkey. He died in 1273.

He was born into a family where spirituality was the ordinary business: his father was a theologian, jurist and mystic, so he was taught his mystical Sufi strand of Islam from a young age. The family moved to Konya when Rumi was a young man. As an adult he prayed for a teacher. And there was a travelling teacher, a dervish called Shams of Tabriz who had prayed for a student to whom he could pass on what he had learned of the spiritual life. They met on 15 November 1244, and that changed Rumi's life.

My love affair with Rumi began with a quote on someone's bathroom door: 'There's a field beyond right and wrong – I'll meet you there.' What an invitation to peace-making! It has been with me ever since. Then a couple of years later at a national spiritual directors' conference, I heard a speaker tell Rumi's life story. His pupil/teacher relationship with Shams had become deep and intense. After four years of this mentoring, Rumi had learned much that led to his spiritual progress. Then Shams disappeared and it is suspected that he was murdered by one of Rumi's two sons. Rumi was heart-broken and went searching for him until the day he realised that the presence and voice of the teacher was within him. This gave him a model for understanding Divine Love. He had a profound experience of this one day in the market and was so overwhelmed by this awareness that he danced his joy by whirling then and there in the street.

Rumi wrote copiously: many books of poems which are sources of wisdom and delight to many spiritual seekers of all faith traditions today. His major work is a six-volume poem considered by many to be one of the greatest works of mystical poetry. It contains about 27,000 lines of poetry. I've heard a concentrated reading of his translated works described as like eating a whole box of liqueur chocolates at once. So much wisdom there, that each piece can give pleasure and opportunity for much savouring and reflection.

This whirling became the pattern of prayer for the order of a strand of Sufism based on his teaching. The order is known today as Mevlevi, after the title Rumi was given – Mevlana, the Complete One. The participants are also known as Whirling Dervishes, an expression which in English at least has acquired a slightly pejorative flavour that includes 'frenzied'. This is a really off-beam interpretation of a profound and moving prayer ceremony. The word 'dervish' means 'threshold' – as in coming to the threshold of mystical experience as one who 'stands at the door'.

I've been privileged to meet with the Wellington-based group of Sufi Turners and have taken part as a prayerful 'watcher' or 'lover' in their ceremony. They are dressed for it in the traditional white robes which signify their burial garments and tall hats which represent their tomb-stones. There is prayer and traditional flute music, and the turning ceremony (sama) begins. The right hand is open to the heavens to receive; the left hand is turned towards earth to give. It is beautiful, tranquil and deeply God-focused and prayerful. The turning continues in various formations round the floor for 30 minutes. The turning lesson I had at an inter-spirituality gathering was special: focusing on the thumb of the leading hand avoids dizziness. The footwork can be easily learnt. Within a few minutes, the sensation was of being the axle, the still point for the turning world. Opening to Divine Love is what it is all about.

Rumi was also an astute student of human nature. His poem fragment 'This being human is a guest house,' anticipates much that is now understood about the therapeutic value of admitting and welcoming one's more uncomfortable emotions. This pre-dated Jung's teaching about embracing one's shadow by several hundred years.

Another favourite poem of mine begins:

> The temple of love is not love itself;
> True love is the treasure, not the walls about it.

He died in 1273 and was buried beside his father. After his death the order of Mevlevi was founded by his son now known as Sultan Veled, and a beautiful mosque built over the tombs along with a complex of dervish cells, dance hall and school. Now this is a museum and a place of pilgrimage for many.

My closest encounter with Rumi happened in 2015 when I was excited to discover a study tour of Turkey would include Konya and a visit to his tomb. For that day I would become a pilgrim, and I talked to various tour-group friends about my passion for Rumi and his writings. From the hotel window we could see the fluted turquoise spire of the mosque. A short walk got us there the next morning. Even with its secularised status, it was still appropriate to be adequately covered, and to put on the supplied blue plastic overshoes before entering. Throngs of Muslim pilgrims, throngs of more western tourists. Not a full mingling, more like a flowing patchwork, each with our own. As we stood before the tomb, I was full of awe at being so close to this saintly man, as well as admiring the intense jewel-coloured panels of Arabic script decorating that corner of the building.

Suddenly someone took my hand and slipped a ring onto my finger. It was a beautiful older Muslim woman who then embraced me, kissed me on both cheeks and disappeared into the crowd. An exquisite gift of Spirit-connection! A reaching out across the faith gap in the spirit of the one we were both honouring. I wasn't the only one astounded and deeply moved by what happened – two of the tour women told me they had had tears in their eyes as they had watched the encounter. And they asked, 'How did she know to pick you?' And one of the men said, 'It makes you think!' The little green ring is proof that it wasn't a dream. If only this reaching over could be universal! But I'm sure that the spirit of Rumi was joyfully watching over us that morning. We had truly met in his field!

Words and Worship

To engage in dialogue means not only questioning one's own assumptions, but also to realise first of all those assumptions exist. One assumption I have learned to question is that people, especially from a different faith or tradition, mean the same thing by a word as I do. This gets in the way of communication, rather than facilitating it. I needed to ponder this as we passed through early November with All Saints, All Souls and the Mexican

> Encountering other traditions meant becoming more aware of the need for respectful explorations of the significance of their terminology – and of my own.

Day of the Dead (Dia de los Muertos). All, one way or another, honouring those who have gone before us.

In other contexts, we call the connection we have with them the Communion of the Saints. That's all of us, those here and those beyond, and celebrating the bond that goes on for always. In a recent conversation about the beliefs of an indigenous minority, I was asked, 'Are they into ancestor-worship?' I wondered in response whether their connection with the departed ones is really much different from the standard Catholic/Christian one. We all, somehow or other, look for wisdom from those who have gone before.

The word 'worship' has caused significant problems over the centuries. In my background this means giving single-minded honour and reverence to the one and only Supreme Deity. So 'worshipping' anything other than God is idolatry. Hence the condemnation by the Reformers and their Protestant successors of the supposed Catholic practice of 'worshipping' Mary and the Saints. We were taught as Catholics that they were quite wrong – that we 'venerated' these holy ones and that was quite different from worship. But why did they think we were 'worshipping'? Because they saw the attention and energy focussed there, they saw the pictures, the statuary, they saw the bowing, the kneeling, the praying – to them all these were signs of 'worship'. But we knew very clearly that was not what was happening. The statues and pictures were akin to the family photo album.

Recently I've become aware that spiritual people in and beyond churches use the word 'worship' as a synonym for the Catholic 'venerate', as simply 'showing reverence to'. When some pilgrimage companions described their kissing an icon of Mary in a Greek church as worship, I was astonished to say the least. Here, apparently, were a bunch of women of assorted spiritualities actually doing what Catholics had been accused of for centuries: 'worshipping' a picture, 'worshipping' Mary.

Only later, by asking the question at the next level down, did I understand their intention. 'When you say 'worship', what do you mean?' Response: 'Showing reverence and recognising the Divine spark.' Then, 'This is what it means to me …' And so to some meaningful dialogue and increased understanding. The missionaries of colonising times were rarely given to those clarifying conversations. Hence the condemnations of indigenous spiritual practices: if people burnt a lamp before images of their ancestors, it was 'worshipping' them; if they had many images of 'gods' with different names, they were polytheistic; if they bowed before and prayed to a sacred rock, tree or carving, they were 'worshipping' idols. And anyway, they were all heathens, pagans and 'wrong', whereas we Christians were 'right'.

Early Christian missionaries accused Hindus of all these misdoings, and more: they 'worshipped' snakes, horrifying to those whose symbol system saw snakes as the embodiment of evil. I heard a story that in India, it was taught that the safest thing to do if confronted by a rearing snake was to bow from the waist and wait. What if this is simply a practice of convincing the snake of meeting one of a superior size, at which it will hopefully turn tail and depart? This bowing could well look like 'worship.' Hindus are clear that there is but one Ultimate Reality, of which all the rest (and maybe even snakes) are but images, symbols or manifestations.

Perhaps what we have all had in common is the use of images as prisms – what is truly being acknowledged is the Ultimate Reality. As prisms break up the white light into separately discernible colours to which we give names, so the human spirit 'breaks up' the Unfathomable into experiences and images that are graspable and nameable by our minds, even as we know their inadequacy. And these varied images are generated in turn by culture and history.

Words are themselves metaphors. If we think of a four-legged creature that moos and gives milk, the reality of its being is not affected by whether it is named in the various languages as cow (English), vache (French), kuh (German), mucca (Italian) etc. The words point to the reality of the animal, but do not share its actual identity. The animal is unchanged by the names. And so, it is with the Holy One, the Divine Presence: namings and their variety do not affect the essence of the Ultimate Reality. Whatever way She/He is named changes only our perception and expectations as we commune in our various ways of prayer.

Sadly, Benedict XVI refused to pray with people of other faith traditions in Assisi, stepping away from the example set by John Paul II 25 years earlier. It seems he hadn't figured out that the Isness Christians call God is the same Reality that others call Allah or Brahman or…

And maybe Colin McCahon could have the last word. In his 1968 painting *Visible Mysteries no 8*, he prays 'Grant that what we have received in visible mysteries, we may obtain in its invisible effects.' Perhaps the various faith traditions can be called 'visible mysteries.' For ourselves and others we pray for the 'invisible effects' – the Wholeness, the Oneness, the Connectedness, the Joy…

The Interfaith Journey

> Reflecting on decades of learning about other maps for the spiritual journey.

Given initiatives in Aotearoa after the 2019 terrorist attack, and the general world need for greater understanding and respect, I've pondered my path of connecting with people of other faiths. Some key experiences are described in my other books, but a brief look at the learnings that have occurred clarifies the journey for me.

In the 1970s and 80s, when I belonged to a Catholic Charismatic lay community, one of our learnings together was exploring Christianity's Jewish roots. We read about their festivals, recognised that several prayers in the Mass had Jewish phrases and origins. We had our own Sabbath meals, the household ceremony of candle-lighting, giving thanks, with the two loaves of bread representing the tablets with the Ten Commandments inscribed, and the shared meal. And we recognised the terrible legacy of the anti-Semitism which had been invented by the Christian Church. Later, a good Jewish friend honoured me with invitations to her family seder – the Passover meal that Jesus ate with his friends the night before he died, and the basis for the Christian Eucharist/Communion. (EP 17)

For a couple of years before my husband's death in 1986, I had belatedly attended Al-Anon, the organisation for families and friends of alcoholics. This was my first experience of a spirituality that was not church-based and had quite different words about living deeply. It didn't take me long to recognise in the 12-Step Programme the basic spiritual disciplines I had grown up with: committing one's life to God, examination of conscience, acknowledging shortcomings to someone else (confession), making amends, and daily prayer or meditation. It was for me almost all about recognising equivalent concepts and dynamics in the new words, which give desperate people tools for coming into the experience of a Power beyond themselves to help deal with their situation. (FE 29)

As a spiritual director in the 1990s, I belonged to a Wellington group that met every couple of months. We were already comfortably interdenominational as Christians from our training. The essence of the individual spiritual journey transcends those definitions and divisions. We decided to visit Temple Sinai, the Jewish Progressive Congregation to ask, 'Please tell us about your faith.' Some of us were more astonished than others by the similarities with Christianity. (FE 113) Then we went to a Buddhist temple, where we found fewer similarities, but still understandings, spiritual practices and ideals in common. Then to the Kilbirnie mosque, and again recognised our common monotheistic roots, stories, practices and ideals. Some of us wanted to continue with a visit to the Hindu temple, but for others the step into a supposedly polytheistic faith tradition was 'a step too far'. I did visit the Hindu temple much later, and there found a baby Krishna in his cradle, having been born at midnight…

I read Bede Griffiths on the similarities between Christianity and Hinduism, and Thomas Merton on those between Christianity and Buddhism. They made so much sense, and I began to see the different faiths as culturally-generated systems of symbols and metaphors. And the need to recognise that different faith traditions both used the same words with differing implications and meanings, and different words for the same ideals, practices and experiences. Careful listening and translation often needed!

A Goddess pilgrimage to Crete in 2006, led by Carol Christ, was another important time that matched my feminist understanding. (EP 72) We were immersed in that ancient matrilineal society's history, Mother Goddess, Earth as Her body as we sat in dark caves, swam in moonlight, and visited mountain-top shrines. I couldn't figure how some of the group could possibly understand Mother Mary as the Goddess. More reading back home, and eventually I got a sense that the very ancient myth of the Primal Mother had landed on this Jewish woman. And a very disconcerting thought

– what if the ancient myth of the dying-and-rising again god-man, son of a virgin mother, had similarly landed on the human Jesus? I put that aside as being irrelevant in practical terms to my relationship with him which has been so central to my life and so enriching.

This was followed by two trips to the feminist Lutheran herchurch in San Francisco, to friends from the Crete pilgrimage for their Divine Feminine conferences. During the visits to that city, I twice danced a spiral with a thousand others, led by NeoPagan witch Starhawk, at the November New Year celebrations of their Reclaiming Community. (EP 86) A magnificent experience!

A week's workshop with shaman John Broomfield was prompted by reading his impressive book *Other Ways of Knowing*, then discovering he's a Kiwi and was living back in Aotearoa New Zealand. We spent time communing with Spirit in nature. Many of the exercises were no different from what we'd done on Catholic retreats. Again, words were important. Terminology was different but I could translate: the shamanic 'spirit guide' meant for me Jesus, shamanic 'journeying' was the same basic process as Ignatian prayer using imagination, 'power animals' equated to guardian angels. Further workshops with him have been equally spiritually rewarding. Also a study tour he led, to be with an Aborigine tribe in Central Australia, added another dimension to my appreciation of indigenous beliefs. (EP 89-90)

As a member of Spiritual Directors International, I was offered an online Inter-spirituality retreat in 2010. SDI is a global organisation with members from 56 faith groups. The administration includes people from all the main faith traditions. Its mission statement is 'Tending the holy around the world'. The structure of the retreat was focus on a topic held in common by all faiths each of the six weeks, e.g. Compassion, Justice, Peace. It was beautifully and movingly obvious that despite clear differences, we shared so much in terms of how to live, how to relate to the Divine and to each other.

The following year, with three others I organised that inter-spirituality retreat described earlier. It was a wonderful time of discovery and connectedness that our local participants and organisers alike deeply appreciated.

Rumi came into my heart with his quotation, 'There's a field beyond right and wrong – I'll meet you there'. I connected with the Sufi community here as related in a previous piece (p. 62). The story I wrote of my encounter with the Muslim woman at his tomb has been a gift. As I've met local Muslim women before and since the March 15 attack, this piece has been a rapport-building gift to offer them. They've been astonished that a Christian would have heard of Rumi, let alone be (slightly) acquainted with his poetry.

Especially since the Christchurch massacre, these women have been active in my area promoting understanding of Islam. There has been a series of community-based information evenings on each of several faiths practised in Aotearoa. They were well attended and good learning for all involved. I found the Sikh evening particularly fascinating as I knew nothing about them beyond their turbans. 'Sikh' means seeker, and we were assured we could be sikhs without being Sikhs. A lot of lovely tolerance for other paths!

A good friendship has developed with one of the Muslim women in particular. We can sit for a couple of hours over coffee, finding out about each other's beliefs and practices. Deep stuff sometimes: how do you pray? Who to? What happens for you? She recently invited me to a Women of Faith meeting, being organised by a Latter-day Saints friend of hers. Accepting the invitation was easy, despite not knowing what the framework or intention would be. It was actually a meeting organised by the women of the Wellington Interfaith Council, supported by the Office of Ethnic Affairs. About 30 women from Islam, Buddhism, Judaism and several versions of Christianity lunched together, then shared their faith in response to the question, 'Where do you find the Light for your life in your tradition?' Then there was a small group brain-storm exercise around questions of how we can carry this womanly collaboration forward in our communities. Friendships are key, as is gentle education in our own circles. And yes please, more connecting as a group.

From these connections I have concluded all these paths are indeed systems of myth, symbols and metaphors for the same path. It is the path of Love, Compassion, Truth-seeking, Justice, Service, devotion to the understanding and service of the Holy Mystery, ourselves, other humans and the planet. The walls between faith traditions are illusory. They are human constructs which have surrounded the central deep Ultimate Reality. As such, they are flawed, and regrettably these flaws are what are visible to outsiders. But within each, the same sacred Mystery and the path to union are preserved. We have so judged each other, so feared being contaminated or misled. Any understanding on a personal level will enhance widening circles of loving respect. When I know what you believe, I understand you better. I don't need to change a thing. Ultimately All is One!

The Pandemic

At the time of writing, mid-July 2020, New Zealand is enjoying a breathing space. There were 24 heady days of no cases of Covid-19 at all in the country, then came the hiccups – four escapes from the quarantine regime for returning Kiwis

Living through history

and new cases caught at the border. We are living fairly normally but know it is a fragile space, in view of the chaos still rampant in much of the rest of the world. Thank God for Prime Minister Jacinda Adern and Dr Ashley Bloomfield who directed the tough stuff that has got us safely to here. Fifteen million cases world-wide and counting. So much tragic nonsense from some world leaders which has even been equated to genocide.

So much about this time has been said so often. I will talk rather about how Covid-19 affected my life. Early on, I told my offspring not to worry if I got it and died. At 78,

I'm comfortable with the fact that I have to die of something sooner or later. I was bemused by all the grocery stock-piling that was going on, despite the assurance that supermarkets were staying open. I did get a couple of tins of soup and long-life milk. When over-70s were told to stay home, there were lots of emailed offers of help flying round our Neighbourhood Support Group of about a dozen homes. I accepted four of these over the five weeks, my dear Muslim friends insisted on doing a stint too as part of their Ramadan practice, and there was the 'goody bag' of food from neighbours who were closing down their café for the duration. I was so grateful for all that!

The four weeks solitude in my much-loved home was quite beautiful. I had always wanted to do a 30-day retreat and here it was. I was of course conscious of the tremendous difficulties and stresses lockdown was causing most other people in the wider community. Apart from a couple of donations to the increasingly crucial foodbanks, the best thing I could do for them was staying in and staying well myself. Keeping in touch with friends and family by phone and Skype was important. Initially there was a swamping deluge of emailed 'helpful' things to read and do. I had to ignore them. But then – all those spacious days with no external responsibilities, gift hours to follow my nose and heart! Some unusual cleaning like skirting boards and cupboards melded with meditation times, daily walks in the gorgeous autumn sun, and creative doings. Writing, two pictures painted, two quilts made for Women's Refuge, lots of reading. A regime I positively thrived on! It was odd to experience it so differently to the prevailing communal story of anxiety, loneliness, frustration, stress and heart-break. Along with others of my peers, I felt intensely privileged to be so insulated!

Online church services were a pleasurable way to keep connected with my parish, as was the weekly newsletter contributed to by all members of our coffee group. My little contributions to that recorded snippets from my diary of the time. They give the flavour of my experience in those weeks:

Things that have given me pleasure:

The early quick, no-contact visit from a good friend with what she described as a 'sanity pack' – a gorgeous huge book and two DVDs.

Someone's pale orange dahlias against their blue plumbago flowers.

A Wilton Bush happening – a ten-minute watch while a fantail shadowed a feeding kaka about one metre away. The kaka walked along branches and creepers from one side of the path to the other, fantail presumably enjoying the disturbed tidbits. A delightful bit of bird behaviour!

An Esplanade happening – a dad and the owner of a dachshund puppy encouraging a toddler to stroke it. Toddler in turquoise hoodie very diffident. Half a dozen on-lookers at 'social distance', me too. Owner knelt down, picked puppy up, toddler eventually did manage a stroke, applause from the on-lookers.

The colours of my lunchtime Vogel's bread topped with avocado and my favourite beetroot chutney.

The planet is breathing more easily. We couldn't or wouldn't do all this pruning for Mother Earth's sake, but are having to do it to save ourselves. I believe this is an evolutionary moment for human beings. Will we hold onto the simplicity when the virus has passed?

More pleasures: watching a yellow admiral butterfly sunning itself on grey pebbles, a bumble bee on a purple thistle flower, a tui on a 5m agave flower stalk – think it's like the ones that had publicity in Auckland a while back. The last beautiful coral rose in my garden – smells lovely. Harvesting three cups of cranberries from my bush before the storm hit. They're like little rubies on my breakfast muesli. To join in the bear-hunt, I remembered my big cuddlesome one. Her name is Edwina, and she's propped by the front window to be spotted by passing families. Sometimes she waves.

I'm noticing that the virus is something of a leveller – homeless people are being put into motels, and Australian professional rugby players are having their salaries chopped from $1,000,000 to 'only' $100,000. Poor things!

Health professionals and supermarket workers all deserve medals.

I figure introverts have some evolutionary advantage in the current situation.

The Prime Minister telling Kiwi children the Easter Bunny and Tooth Fairy are essential workers, but may not get round everywhere. I'm glad she gets a few lighter moments.

Grey warblers' songs nearly every time I walk. How does such a tiny bird let loose such a cascade of joyful notes? And with almost no traffic, a real live venturesome Easter Bunny on roadside grass, a toddler watching it, entranced. I watched them both.

The Good Friday TV interview with the Kiwi paramedic in New York facing possible death from the virus rather than 'running away home'. Love in action.

USA friends beside themselves with horror at Donald Trump's doings. He should talk to Boris Johnson who was a minimiser till it nearly killed him.

Enjoyed a few ripe cape gooseberries from my bush. They come in such lovely little lanterns. Satisfaction at referring another friend who had gone phone-less for five weeks to useful high-up telco bod. She's now connected, but it's been very difficult for her. Good phone chats to friends, St Andrew's and others. Happy Skypes with grandchildren.

The funeral went beautifully on Thursday. Because it was just nine available close family members and me, the family found it very intimate and more relaxed than if there had been a large crowd. They sent out a lovely full order of service to other family and close friends here and overseas before the service so they could work through it as we did. Their experience was very different to the general attitude to current funeral limits.

My granddaughter should have had her graduation ceremony on Thursday for her BA with the A+ average. I'd hoped she'd wear her great-great-grandmother's 1902 academic hood from Glasgow under her own. Maybe at the catch-up ceremony.

As a contact-free greeting, Namaste is much more respectful and dignified than bumping elbows. The Divine in me acknowledges the Divine in you.

A toddler, out walking with his dad, who just laughed and laughed. I had to as well as I overtook them. Joy is so catchy! My huge azalea bush opposite my front door is ablaze with pink spring, the green hellebore are opening, and even crazier, there's a little bunch of strawberries ripening, one already quite red. In May!

Eventually we were let out to be carefully normal. A pang of dismay at the end of my blissful season of hermitting. What I'd missed most were hugs and walks on my favourite beach. Relief for those wanting to get their businesses up and running again.

Community was so important. The PM's constant reminders of Kindness and that we were being a Team of 5 Million built a sense of unity. As everyone was out walking, carefully observing social distancing, we spoke to each other. There was huge kindness being shared around. Hopefully connections forged and strengthened during this time will carry on into the future. Will the planet that got to breathe easily for a while get choked again? Or will the lessons learned reinforce the positive changes?

The best summary I have seen of Covid-19 times, produced by a young Kiwi guy in UK, is here:

> https://www.thenational.ae/arts-culture/books/the-great-realisation-why-this-british-writer-s-pandemic-poem-caught-the-eye-of-jake-gyllenhaal-1.1015262

It is so moving!

> And then, in mid-August, after our 100 case-free days, there has been another outbreak in Auckland. Work to contain it, the upping of alert levels, cancellations, yet another graduation postponement, face-masks, delayed general election. We've done it before. We can do it again! It seems the Covid-19 virus will possibly be in the world with us for years, or until a vaccine is created.

Love and Social Justice

Love and Social Justice

Some years of poverty, followed by time as a long-term beneficiary alongside minimal employment gave me a small taste of life on the other side of society, and a passion to be with those whose situations were immeasurably more difficult than mine. Sometimes this has meant being an interpreter to those of goodwill whose lives haven't intersected with the harder stories, and advocacy with those who have power. I have generally been an accompanier/supporter rather than a communal activist for change. The long-ago words of a priest have proven true: 'If you want to meet God, go to the poor.' I have learned so much from people who have been marginalised by church and society.

I honour the Catholic Social Justice teaching which I absorbed in my 50+ years in that context. 'God's preferential option' for the marginalised is preached but officially practised only selectively. A significant factor in my eventual departure from the Church was the tragic lack there of practising it internally. All the exclusions and self-preserving tactics! I came to call the prioritising of church rules over the Gospel 'ecclesiolatry' – worship of the institution. The Vatican is not the only church institution guilty of this.

My two foundational texts for involvement in Social Justice are Luke 4:16-19 where Jesus quotes the Isaiah text on freeing the people at the bottom of the social heap, and the Kairos Document which emerged from apartheid-era South Africa. The other main thread is power analysis – looking at gender, economic status, education, role and other markers – and choosing to stand with those with least power. These combine to make my understanding of Liberation Theology.

'Love one another as I have loved you.'

Pentecost Prayer

Luke 4:16-21

Written for a Social Justice writers' hui.

(Can be read by various voices)
To me too is God's Spirit given. [Pause]
Response: May I be radically open to receive this Pentecost gift of Spirit.
Silence

For I too am anointed. [Pause]
Response: May I accept and live this empowerment. [Silence]

I too am sent to give good news to the poor. [Pause]
Response: May I understand more deeply my own poverty, and the good news that I matter. [Silence]

I too am sent to proclaim liberty to captives. [Pause]
Response: May I understand more deeply all that is captive within myself and seek God's liberty. [Silence]

I too am sent to proclaim to the blind new sight. [Pause]
Response: May my eyes be freed from all that limits my vision, so that I might see justice as God sees. [Silence]

I too am sent to set the downtrodden free. [Pause]
Response: May I seek freedom for any parts of myself that have been downtrodden by me or by others. [Silence]

I too am sent to proclaim God's unconditional love. [Pause]
Response: May I know God's deep healing in myself, so that with deep personal conviction I may offer hope and challenge to others. [Silence]

Being A Neighbour

A *Refresh* topic[50]

Many years ago I watched a series of videos from a US university on the Table Ministry of Jesus. This was a new concept for me, but it made so much sense. Who did Jesus choose to eat with? The B team, the shunned, socially unacceptable ones, tax-collectors and sinners. Whom did he ask for a drink of water? The B team Samaritan woman. Whose memory did he say would be honoured down the generations? The B team woman who was forgiven much because she loved much. Jesus was a neighbour to them, joining them in their world, and they were neighbours to him. And his explicit teaching that the despised Samaritan who helped the wounded traveller was the one who was the neighbour. Not that the gospel story continues this far, but it's good to imagine that the injured traveller was overwhelmed with gratitude for the help he was given, and once he'd recovered was able to contribute somehow to his benefactor's well-being, and also to pass it forward to another in need.

The concept of 'neighbour' has a great deal to do with willingness to offer hospitality. This may not necessarily involve inviting people to a physical meal, or bandaging physical wounds, but having the open eyes, ears and heart which invite others to be fully present with you for longer or shorter times. It's about paying attention, noticing, really seeing the other, the neighbour, and conveying, 'I see you, and you matter'. About actively including, not excluding, the stranger, the waifs and strays, the other.

I think of four life-affirming movies, all with a deep spiritual message of being 'neighbour', sometimes played out as at odds with the non-life-giving organised religion in their environment. There's *Babette's Feast* (1987), where a whole inheritance is spent on one meal for a community who despite living together for years are still strangers, suspicious of and antagonistic towards each other. During the meal, they opened their hearts to each other. And *Antonia's Line* (1995), where her table for celebrations gets longer and longer as all the misfits, 'sinners' and B team members are serially included with acceptance and respect. And *Chocolat* (2000), where again the heroine's unconditional acceptance and support work miracles in the lives of the town's strugglers. In all three there was hospitality, neighbourliness that healed.

A more recent movie, *Pride* (2014), is the parable of the Good Samaritan writ large into our own times and culture. The despised 'others', the 'Samaritans', were a group of London gay and lesbian friends who decided to support the striking miners of the Welsh village because they themselves knew what it was like to be ostracised and victimised. They gave unconditional love and support, despite rejections and struggles, the crucifixion of seeming failure, and for one a literal death sentence. Eventually, when it all seemed to be over, there was the turn-around that made legal history as Trade Unions abandoned their discriminatory homophobic policies and gave acceptance and exponential reciprocal support to those who had initiated the relationship. It made powerful viewing. Getting to know each other as good-hearted human beings was the key. 'Who,' Jesus still asks, 'were the neighbours to the ones in need?'

The cosmos, our planet and all its creatures too are our neighbours and have needs to be tended. To serve the well-being of a hurting Earth, we can choose to reduce our own ways of harming it, however benign they seem from day to day. We can eat, dress and play less lavishly, so we can reduce our impact on the environment, and give more to those with greater needs.

In the internal dimension, welcoming, loving and supporting the wounded, B team parts of oneself can be a real challenge. Christian programming has traditionally urged us to suppress, disown, ignore, malign as sinful these inconvenient, disreputable and elements of one's self. To know God's healing, we're actually invited to be a compassionate neighbour to these parts of ourselves as well. That way life can be a lot less of a battle. 'Know thyself' is a wise saying that pre-dated Christianity, but still applies. How much more compassionate it is to realise that our own unskilful behaviours (and those of others) come from woundedness, from life wounds that need bandaging and gentle tending so that they can heal. Without self-care and appropriate self-love (not to be confused with selfishness), our energy for being a neighbour will be severely undermined and limited.

So all that exists is my neighbour. Nothing and no-one can be excluded. The 'how' of it can be much more complex. There are times where it is better in the long term to stand back to leave people with the responsibility for steering their own lives, times where a power analysis of a situation means standing with those with less rather than those with more, times where the truly loving thing is to say 'No'. It can often be for me a greater challenge to figure how to be a neighbour to the rich and powerful.

Being a neighbour is meant to be a life-consuming commitment for followers of Jesus. The world's needs often seem overwhelming. I had a beloved and wise mother-in-law. Her philosophy was simple: Do the work that's nearest!

Being a neighbour is the task of faith communities as well as of individual pilgrims. This is where the table-ministry of Jesus is – or isn't – at its most evident. How many parishes speak the words on Sundays, 'Wherever you have come from, wherever you are going, whatever you believe, whatever you don't believe, you are welcome at this table'?

Just Peace

For any peace to last it has to be based on justice.

A Refresh topic[51]

In the early 1980s when apartheid was still alive and well, over 150 South African theologians of various denominations and both races sat together to work out a Christian and biblical response to the institutional injustice that prevailed and that caused such enormous suffering.

In 1985, they issued the *Kairos Document*. The 'Kairos' in the title is a Greek word meaning 'the time is now' or the 'sacred (or propitious) moment'. This document has had enormous effects on my thinking about violence of all sorts, including domestic violence, and the range of Godly responses possible. Their analysis was actually quite shocking to someone brought up on Christianity equalling mandatory forgiveness, peace and reconciliation, no matter what the outcome.

After critiquing what they call State Theology, where effectively 'might is right', the theologians then discuss the uselessness of standard Church Theology against institutional oppression such as they lived with. Forgiveness, peace and reconciliation of themselves cannot produce a just peace. Efforts of that sort change nothing, unless the perpetrators of the injustice have a miraculous, corporate and extremely unlikely change of heart.

So the theologians move on to outline a Prophetic Theology, where they say those who are oppressed have the responsibility to take action to resist oppression. Advice and teaching to simply keep on forgiving does not grow the Shalom of God. They describe as 'sin' any attempt, 'to persuade those of us who are oppressed to accept our oppression and become reconciled to the intolerable crimes committed against us'. And, 'like Jesus, we must expose this false peace'. As disciples, 'we should promote truth and justice and life at all costs, even at the cost of creating conflict, disunity and dissensions along the way...' (in a domestic violence context, marriages may break up as a result). 'If the oppressor does introduce reforms that might lead to real change, this will come about because of a strong pressure from those who are oppressed. True justice, God's justice, demands a radical change of structures. This can only come ... from the oppressed themselves.'

Oppression, they say, is the experience of, 'being crushed, degraded, humiliated, exploited, impoverished, defrauded, deceived, enslaved'. Strong words, readily recognizable in the former experience of black South Africans, but how easily do we recognize this as the experience of the woman next door, or of parishioners we sit with on Sunday mornings?

> 'It cannot be taken for granted that everyone who is oppressed has taken up their own cause and is struggling for their own liberation. Nor can it be assumed that all oppressed Christians are fully aware that their cause is God's cause.... The Church must then help people understand their rights and duties. There must be no misunderstanding about the moral duty of all who are oppressed to resist oppression and to struggle for liberation and justice'.

Here is a call for a peace based on God's justice. It has pastoral applications way beyond the intended situation of apartheid in South Africa. The call by women around the world for justice and equality was already well underway when the *Kairos Document* was issued. Since then, in Aotearoa New Zealand there has been protest by Māori about the injustices done to them and some progress has been made. The Disabled have made their needs known and again there has been some progress. Their slogan 'Nothing about us without us' is a potent reminder that people, all people, are entitled to a voice in making justice. Most recently Gay, Lesbian, Bisexual, Transgender and Intersex communities have demanded and received more equal rights under the law. Deprivation of 'the other' of their rights by a more powerful group or institution can never be justified. Jesus was the Great Includer. The more marginalized people were, the closer he chose to be to them. Shalom, the 'Kin-dom', the Realm of God – true peace based on justice – is better served by resistance to oppression rather than a martyred submission.

> The spirit of the Lord has been given to me
> for he has anointed me.
> He has sent me to bring good news to the poor,
> to proclaim liberty to captives
> and to the blind new sight,
> to set the downtrodden free,
> and to proclaim the Lord's year of favour.
>
> *Luke 4:18*

A Closure

It's nearly bedtime and I'm tired. It is the Friday in Passion Week. Today has been extraordinary. With others I have been living the way of the Cross right now.

This morning I sat with a group of people whose workplace was going out of existence today. They belonged to Mana Recovery, an award-winning charitable trust which for 19 years has supported the rehabilitation of people with mental health issues. Some had dual diagnoses of intellectual disability as well. Some would have had criminal convictions if it hadn't been for their diagnosable illnesses. In a strange sense, they were the lucky ones. They were sufficiently mentally ill to be not in prison.

> This and the two following pieces were written at the 2015 sad funding-driven end of Mana Recovery where I had been the chaplain for 18 years.[52]

Mana Recovery was initiated in 1996 with the closure of the long-stay wards at Porirua psychiatric hospital, and developed into a work skills programme around light assembly work and recycling of mostly plastic and paper. There were also literacy and life-skills education, and art lessons which facilitated the flowering of an extraordinary range of talents, as witnessed in a wonderful art exhibition in 2011. Such healing! Better than many medical solutions.

When people had recovered sufficiently, many were employed in real paid jobs in the organisation: they were 'off the benefit', 'normal', and at last free from all the hassles and requirements of Work and Income (WINZ). Last year new mental health strategies meant that the District Health Board (DHB) axed the funding to a number of mental health-related agencies. Mana Recovery has not been the only one to close as a result.

I have been privileged to spend most of its years as workplace chaplain to Mana Recovery. It has been a profound journey of learning the wisdom, courage, generosity, sense of community and the compassion that the trainees and supported staff have had amongst themselves. Some of them have been in the system for 30 years. They know each other very well. I came to understand that if I had had the horrific childhood experiences that some of them had, I too could have become ill, violent, deprived, devastatingly marginalised.

There was the one many years ago who told me he'd been introduced to glue sniffing when he was seven and that from then on he called his glue bag, 'My mummy'. The one who was so proud that he'd learned to tell the time as an adult and who worked hard on sorting the recycling because, 'It keeps the sea cleaner and saves the fishes.' The ones who had been sent as little intellectually handicapped boys to a Catholic institution where they were sexually abused and who were still having nightmares 40 years later. The women who were raped, in or out of hospital. The ones with profound, if not always healthy, religious beliefs. And many more.

My simply being around for a few hours a week, and eventually accepted as someone who could be talked with was useful for both staff and trainees. In many ways, I had the easy job. The staff were the ones who had to manage the day-to-day well-being of the clients, including the inevitable regular challenging behaviours and infrequent angry outbursts. The trainees, as we called them, could be their best selves with me, and that had its value.

Specifically spiritual conversations only happened if initiated by a trainee. If there was a death, and there were many over the years, we would have a karakia time to remember the person and the others who'd gone before, to pray for them, and for peace and comfort for those who were left. They'd wonder who would be next. They probably hadn't read the statistics that say mental health clients have on average 15 years lower life expectancy than the general population, but they knew they were vulnerable. In recent years, the requests for a karakia time grew more regular till we were having one each week.

Up to a dozen of us would gather, and after saying a brief introductory prayer, always focusing simply on God's unconditional love for them personally, I'd invite them to speak their own prayers. Some with church backgrounds were very comfortable doing so, more reticent ones might eventually venture a prayer. It was always moving. One might pray for an ill parent who had always supported her or him. Another would grieve for a long-estranged family. Another asked for courage in dealing with an abusive flatmate. Another prayed for, 'People worse off than us.'

Then there'd be a short discussion on, for example, how having friends helped, and what it might mean to have Jesus for a friend. Some good bonds grew between those who attended. It could still be challenging, though – 'My pastor says I have a demon of schizophrenia. Will you exorcise me?' 'I can't do that, sorry, but I can pray for peace and healing for you. It might be good to get your meds checked soon'; 'I want to say the Catholic prayers, not the Protestant prayers… Hail Mary, full of grace…' That took a bit of ecumenical tact! 'God loves all sorts of prayers and pray-ers.'

Some got better slowly and moved on to independent employment. Many couldn't. And now this training unit and the lawn-mowing one have closed for good. Trash

Palace, Mana Recovery's recycling shop where more people are employed, will be gone in a month. There may be some good-hearted employers out there who can give supported employment to people who can work hard but have variable health. That would be wonderful. Managers and the dedicated Board of Trustees members who have seen the agency through many crises over the years would sleep better if this seemed easily predictable. No-one would be actually willing to bet on it happening for all those affected.

So today, we sat together for a while. I gave each one two tea-light candles. We lit one to represent our life in that building and we shared our good memories, then we lit the second candle to represent our lives beyond today and extinguished the first one. That part of life is over. There will be a future, unforeseeable as it is at the moment. I spoke of Easter and the hope for the new, the unexpected. It is the jobs that have become redundant. People never are. Tears, fears, hugs, hope, partings.

A letter in this morning's *Dominion Post* in response to the announced closure made a succinct point: 'Yet another blow for the people on struggle street who deserve as much support as possible. I wonder how many 'golden handshakes' to departing health board CEOs could have been better directed to helping the real people in our society. The 'hard knocks' these people experience through life just keep on knocking.'

Indeed! While I deeply believe in 'God's preferential option for the poor', right now the people affected by the closure of this agency are travelling the hard road of the Cross. It's not easy to imagine what their Easters might look like, or when they might eventuate. I recognise my suffering Jesus there, my God in their lives, my Eucharist in their sharing of a broken sandwich and stories of broken lives. I am grateful to all I've met at Mana Recovery. They have enriched my life and my faith. I wish I could gather them all, as a mother hen gathers her chicks, and protect them all from their imminent extra hardships. I offer my helplessness to join with theirs and acknowledge the God who weeps with the poor.

Sue's Tooth

A personal lesson in White Privilege

Sue (not her real name) attended Mana Recovery's (MR) skills development programme for mental health consumers for about nine years. She was an extremely hard worker, and her schizophrenia was sufficiently stabilised for her to be given full-time employment on the minimum wage at Trash Palace, which MR had set up for the purpose of providing employment to consumers. She is Māori.

Mana Recovery was an award-winning community trust based in Porirua and gave many people a safe and respectful place to discover and rediscover their mana and usefulness. The withdrawal of District Health Board funding forced its closure in April

2015, along with that of Trash Palace. About a dozen mental health consumers who had been employed no longer were, and virtually all resumed life 'on the benefit'. My educated guess is that it costs WINZ more to pay them benefits, than it would have cost the DHB to keep MR in existence. A true buck-passing!

Anyway, the tooth. After the closure had been announced, there was the worry for staff of what they'd do next, intensified by the awareness that any other sort of employment was highly unlikely. One day a manager told me Sue had a bad tooth-ache and asked if I could help. I checked in with Sue about the options. She had rung the free hospital dental service but had been told she wasn't eligible because she was employed and had (heroically) saved $300. She was scared to ask WINZ for help because she thought they would make her spend the savings before giving her anything. And unemployment was just around the corner.

'It's ok,' she said, 'I'll get over it. It will settle down.' The manager and I would not settle for this, so I took her to WINZ, asked whether she'd like to explain the situation, or whether she wanted me to do it. 'You do it'. So I did. Brilliant! Just go to the dentist next door, get a quote, and come back, we will fund what is necessary. And no, you don't have to spend your savings.' Did that. An abscess was diagnosed, needing immediate extraction. It would not have 'settled down.' Back to WINZ with the quote, filled in the forms, back to the dentist, got the work done and the prescription for antibiotics. Delivered the invoice back to WINZ.

'There,' I said to Sue, 'it worked out fine, didn't it? WINZ were really helpful after all.' Her reply stunned me: 'You're white!' Had it really made a difference? Her experience said 'Yes.'

Mana Recovery closed. When I next had news of her, she had been seen wandering drunk round the streets.

Stretching

Twice in a week it happened, a painful stretch between the pleasure and beauty of human existence and the deep and awful agony of it.

> Privilege underlined

The first time was when I'd enjoyed a good movie with a friend, and we were going to go for a cheap bite and conversation before parting. I've got used to passing the sad beggars through Wellington's main drag. I know there are options for accessing food and shelter through various agencies run by compassionate people. I send them a silent prayer of encouragement and love. Is that enough? I'm still confused about that. So that was how I was attending to the Māori man we were passing as he sat on the concrete steps with the usual scrawled cardboard pleas. A heart acknowledgement, but without really looking at him.

Then he spoke: 'Hello, Trish'. That stopped me in my tracks! I knew the face, I'd have retrieved the name given a minute, but he told me – it was one of the men from Mana Recovery, the mental health agency that closed last Easter after funding cuts. We talked. He's homeless and living rough on the town belt. As always, he was beautifully spoken and courteous. I asked if he knew about one of the agencies that focus on homelessness. Yes, he did, and he goes there. I gave him enough for a meal, and moved on, heart-sick and angry.

Mental Health funding, despite government protestations that it has increased, has been inadequate to sustain agencies that were doing a good job in providing mental health consumers with purpose, safety, companionship and supervision. And then has had the gall to suggest 'Social Bonds' – the provision of just such services based on private investment! The economics of the closure of Mana Recovery and its recycling shop Trash Palace, which also provided employment for those sufficiently stable to commit to work, are bizarre. The DHB saved the money that would have enabled the agency to continue, but effectively passed an even larger bill parcel to WINZ which now has a dozen or more unemployment benefits to pay to people who realistically are unlikely to find other employment.

The second experience was when I went to see whether I could get a last-minute ticket to a World of Wearable Art performance. A visit in a previous year had left me ecstatic about human creativity and ingenuity, the sheer beauty of the creations, and the fizzing energy, joy and fun of the extraordinary staging. Queues of people of all ages buzzed with anticipation, many dressed in their own glamorous contributions to the occasion. It would have been lovely to become part of the excitement, but the only available ticket was well out of my price range. I wasn't too disappointed as the spring sunshine invited a walk along the waterfront, a different sort of pleasure.

Along the way I went – for a miniscule admission price – to see the 2015 prize-winning World Press Photo exhibition. There the other world was writ large and poignantly. A few inspiring and hopeful images, but most depicting the horrors of life for far too many human beings caught in warfare and tragedy in other parts of the world. There was the delirious man with Ebola who had escaped from the hospital and was being hauled up by two treatment personnel in full protective gear. The utterly traumatised face of a teenage girl on hands and knees, injured in a riot. The man in Ukraine in shock after a passenger's body from the shot-down aircraft had plummeted through his roof into his bedroom. A performing monkey cowering from the whip of its owner. A military chaplain holding up a cross for battle-ready troops.

The emotional and spiritual stretch between these two extremes of pleasure and pain, the WOW experience and these photos, was hard to hold. On the one hand … on the other hand … all real, all human. Gratitude that we are so blessed in this imperfect land to be away from the worst of the violence, and – for some – to have space in life for the joyous, the creative. Heartache for those whose daily life is simply trying to survive, both here and world-wide. I recognised eventually the image of the crucifixion, the stretching of the Cross. Resurrection will come, somehow, somewhere. Can we be willing to do the stretching by holding – being with – both extremes, not ignoring either? Can we co-create resurrections for others and for ourselves by the small gestures of compassion and human care along our daily routes? Can we believe with Easter hope that something new and beautiful can grow out of tragedy, that harrowing experiences can be redeemed? This is the challenge, the invitation of our faith.

Listen, love, respect! Justice for Same-sex Couples

> This was my contribution to another of the Catholic Theology books, *But is it Fair? Faith Communities and Social Justice* (2014)

Judeo-Christian-based societies have until recently regarded homosexual people as criminals, perverts, and sinners. In Aotearoa New Zealand official change to this began with the 1986 Homosexual Law Reform Act. Both this and the recent Marriage Amendment Act were strongly opposed by churches.

With this in mind, I offer the experiences of two pioneering faith communities, one Catholic, one Progressive Presbyterian, both of whom almost 30 years ago did the theological reflecting that enabled them to move from the traditional bible-based condemnations of homosexuality to an overt gospel-based acceptance of the lives and loving relationships of homosexual people. My own conversion journey was similar, and I was privileged to be mentored as an AIDS Foundation volunteer by Sister Paula Bretkelly when my work as an industrial chaplain took me into that environment.

Sisters of St Joseph of Nazareth
The Sisters of St Joseph of Nazareth, based in Whanganui, engaged in a focused renewal process from the late 1960s as directed by Vatican II. In the 1980s they had training as a group in the acceptance of diversity and the valuing of difference. Mindful of the gospel call and their congregation's charism to be with the poor and marginalised, they gradually withdrew from teaching in schools to work in areas of greater social need. What eventuated were women who felt called to different areas of work, whose calls were discerned then blessed and missioned by the community. Two, for example, became involved in prison chaplaincy, one trained as a psychotherapist, one is working with whanau up the Whanganui River, others are working on ecological issues and two went as volunteers to the AIDS Foundation.
In the late 1980s people with HIV/AIDS were the lepers of the day – despised, condemned, avoided, and feared. It was to this group that Wellington-based Paula Brettkelly went as a volunteer and gave the next 20 years of her life and ministry. She went armed only with a gospel willingness to listen, love, respect, and learn – despite

'having been brought up', as were the majority of Catholics in those days, to 'despise'[8] homosexual people. She became a light for all those whose lives were darkened more by societal attitudes than by the actual, and at that time always fatal, disease. She listened to the stories of their lives – of rejections, of violent attacks from gay-haters, of the experiences of 'I always knew I was different', of gay siblings and relations. And the stories of the parents – 'I'm supposed to think my son is a perverted, sinful, evil person – but he's not actually like that, he's good! I love and accept him as he is. And his partner.'

Paula served the people at the AIDS Foundation Āwhina Centre as Education and Human Rights officer. She learned their necessarily earthy language and spoke it without embarrassment, validated their lived realities, and when trust had been earned, prayed with the living and the dying, and understood the realities of their lives. She became a staunch defender of the Lesbian, Gay, Bisexual, Transgender, Intersex (LGBTI) communities' right to fairness from the wider community. This included making a submission to the Select Committee supporting Civil Unions in 2004 – and celebrating with gay couples when it was passed and they were finally able to celebrate publicly their committed loves of sometimes many decades standing. Despite ill-health she went on to work at the Human Rights Commission. She was honoured with Membership of the NZ Order of Merit for community work in 2007, nominated by the AIDS Foundation.

When she died in 2008 there was a wonderful memorial service in a full St Joseph's in Wellington: gays, lesbians, transgender people, women from the Prostitutes Collective, nuns, and the 'straight' who all acknowledged being touched by the love and acceptance she had shown to so many. Over refreshments later, some acknowledged they were in a church for the first time in many years, and that they came with significant trepidation. Such places had not been safe for them in the past. It was a gospel gathering where Jesus would have been at home. As he recognisably was.

Paula would be the first to acknowledge that this ministry grew out of her formation as a 'Black Jo' and was sustained by the constant support of her community. They journeyed with her as she moved from the traditional condemnation and the current official Catholic conditional acceptance ('You are ok, as long as you are celibate') to a fearful willingness to understand, then through listening and prayerful discernment to full acceptance of those with HIV/AIDS and the wider gay and lesbian communities as beloved of God.

Sisters Catherine Shelton, Noelene Landrigan and Colleen Woodcock who entered the novitiate with Paula in the 1960s, remembered some significant shifts in their communal understanding of the gospel mandate to love your neighbour. Even in the restrictive days of the 1960s when the vow of obedience was interpreted more literally, they were taught that disobedience was a moral imperative if to obey transgressed the law of charity. In their theological reflections over the years, they embraced successively liberation theology, feminist analysis, revision of their relationships with indigenous people, and those of other faiths. The new understanding of human sexuality and orientations was a further challenge along the same continuum. Liberation theology is based on Jesus' sermon in Luke 4:18 promising freedom for the oppressed and new sight for the blind and has recently been validated by Pope Francis[9] with his focus on the poor.

Modern exegesis and Scripture study throughout these years often threw a different light upon texts, hitherto taken literally. As ecclesial women, the Sisters would not dismiss or teach contrary to the official teaching of the Church, but pastorally often felt called to look beyond the letter of the law to the person – impelled by the gospel imperative to love, to be with and be converted by the marginalised, to accept and value the lived reality of each person. They understand their role within the Church and society as liminal and prophetic, a role which calls them when necessary to critique the values and structures of both – to be, like the prophets of old, the 'loyal opposition'. The focus of their call has always been towards greater love, greater openness to diversity, wider recognition of God at work in the world. Rather than the 'who is in, and who is out?' mentality of orthodoxy, they recognise the presence of the sacred in the lives of all others alongside whom they journey.[10] They understand discernment to have personal, vocational, and community aspects, and that the movement of individuals and the communities to a deeper understanding of the Great Commandment to love constitutes an ongoing process of conversion.

Two quotations sum up the fruitfulness of the ministry of Paula and her community: A woman from a strip club – 'When Paula comes in here, I feel as though I have the right to access God.' And a gay man – 'Your vow of celibacy adds a dimension to my loving.' Through her they had experienced Divine Love. And it was mutual – she began to say, 'My God is gay, black, and beautiful'.[11]

St Andrew's on The Terrace
St Andrew's on The Terrace is a faith community that has lived its journey of gospel inclusivity very publicly in the centre of Wellington, along the way incurring the opposition of the majority of the Presbyterian Church and of some other Christian denominations. In 1979 St Andrew's was declared an 'open door' church, without labels, open to the community and ecumenism. Later, a notice was attached to the outside wall proclaiming, 'Declared to be an inclusive church on 8th December 1991. Including all people of every creed, race, class and sexual orientation.' And there is a rainbow, symbol of hope and diversity.

The community discernment process to reach this declaration was led by the Very Rev John Murray, minister there from 1975 to 1993. He was convinced that openness to the Spirit and the world was the call of the parish. The declaration received significant attention in the media: John Murray was reported as saying, 'As an inclusive church, St Andrew's would be an accepting community for all who feel rejection within the Presbyterian Church or elsewhere, especially at this time for all gay and lesbian Christians and their families and friends.'[12]

Rev Murray describes the process of his own broadening of understanding as, 'a long process of coming to inclusivity, continuing conversion … the struggle of all life. God is relationship – lack of relationship is lack of God. The Gospel and the world engaged together become the Kingdom.' Formative experiences for him as a younger minister were working towards ecumenism, and having to face points of division and rejection, then broadening from ecclesial to social justice issues; as a university chaplain hearing the pain of young gays and lesbians; and knowing a minister's family where four of the six children came out as gay and lesbian, and so recognising a genetic factor in sexual orientation. He had supported Homosexual Law Reform (1986) and had ordained as an elder a well-respected gay member of his congregation. The other members of his community followed this lead in building up a community of the rejected in the Way of Jesus. For some it was just too challenging, and they left.[13]

He believes hearing the stories of real people and hearing Jesus in the stories, is the easier road to change of heart. Changed thinking/theology follows. In our getting to know real people, God facilitates positive changes in relationships that are otherwise blocked by fear, and cultural and religious constraints. There is only fear and love. A choice must be made.

St Andrew's went on to host the second national conference of Gay and Lesbian Christians in 1992, the first time for many participants that they had been able to acknowledge the fullness of who they are in a church. Subsequently, a monthly service was held for gays, lesbians, their friends and families and those who had lost loved ones to AIDS, by a network known as Galaxies (Gay and Lesbian Xtians). It describes itself as a 'spiritual family for LGBTI people'.

The rift in the Presbyterian Church on the acceptability of LGB people in ministry, let alone their marriages, is exemplified by two motions – About Human Sexuality and Church Leadership – to the 1991 General Assembly. The first was sponsored by a minister formerly part of St Andrew's parish.

From the Presbytery of Gisborne:

> WHEREAS all significant medical and psychological information points to the fact that sexual orientation for any individual is formed and fixed by early childhood and is not by free choice, and that it cannot be changed except in rare circumstances.
>
> It is hereby Overtured that the General Assembly:
>
> Affirm that human sexuality is a beautiful and precious gift of God our Creator and enhancing of loving relationships.
>
> Affirm that we are all made in the image of God, and that salvation in Christ is possible for all human beings regardless of their sexual orientation and practice.

> Affirm that sexual behaviour that is demeaning and abusive, and that lacks mutuality and loving care is sinful.
>
> Declare that sexual orientation and consequent mutual loving behaviour is not a bar to ordination or to positions of leadership in the church or to membership in the church.

And in contrast:

From the Presbytery of the Bay of Plenty:

> It is hereby Overtured that the General Assembly:
>
> Affirm that Holy Scripture indicates that homosexual acts are not part of God's loving will for any individual.
>
> Re-affirm that all homosexual acts are sinful.
>
> Specify that open and unrepentant commission of homosexual acts, or public advocacy or condoning of any homosexual acts as acceptable, be a bar to ordination as elder or minister in the Presbyterian Church of New Zealand and a bar to the induction of any person into a position of leadership in the Presbyterian Church of New Zealand.[14]

This conflict, discussed almost yearly since then, is ongoing in the light of the new legislation. Opposing groups disagree passionately about whether or not ministers should have a conscience option on celebrating marriages for same-sex couples.

In 2002 St Andrew's practised its proclamation of inclusivity by calling Rev Dr Margaret Mayman, who happened to be a lesbian, to be its new minister. The 'practice what you preach' ethos has continued with full parish support for the Civil Union Act (2004) and the Marriage Amendment Act (2013). Civil union and marriage celebrations take place there, sometimes including Catholic partners who are unable to be given this acceptance and hospitality by their home parishes.

Conclusion

So what are the common theological threads in the conversion stories of these two communities? Their thinking changed in a prayerful response to the decision to value difference of all sorts, along with actual relationships with LGBTI people. The acceptance and valuing of people of non-heterosexual orientations was another step along a continuum that had included renewal and re-visioning of the Christian call to integrate liberation theology through ecumenism, feminism, awareness of racial inequality, disabilities, interfaith relationships, peace-making, and care for the earth. It is a continuum based on the gospel mandate to love, especially those who suffer from discrimination and marginalisation. The Bible texts traditionally interpreted literally as condemning homosexuality and homosexual people are set aside as less imperative than the call to love, and as products of historical and cultural contexts that are no longer relevant. What facilitated and anchored the new beliefs was hearing the stories of personal and family experiences, and the recognition of real goodness/Godness, in 'the other'. Discernment was actively done at three levels: personal, vocational, and communal. For both communities this has caused sometimes painful conflicts with their governing churches. They both sense a call to be prophetic communities, on the margins themselves through their obedience to a call higher than ecclesiastical teachings. In this they are in solidarity with the marginal ones to whom they minister and who in turn minister to them. They look towards the time when, 'All may be one.'[15]

Internationally known hymn-writer Shirley Murray's new verse for her A *Place at the Table*,[16] written at the request of the St Andrew's parish in 2012, sums it all up

> For gay and for straight, a place at the table,
> a covenant shared, a welcoming space,
> a rainbow of race and gender and colour,
> for gay and for straight, the chalice of grace.
>
> And God will delight when we are creators
> of justice and joy, compassion and peace:
> yes, God will delight when we are creators
> of justice, justice and joy.

The Living Wage Movement

> The labourer is worthy of her/his hire. (Luke 10:7)

A record of a 2018 training event for community activists.[53]

'The working poor' is sadly becoming a familiar phrase in Aotearoa New Zealand.

On 13 May 2019 the Hamilton bus-drivers with the support of their union went on strike to demand the then Living Wage of $20.55 per hour. This is the 2018 figure which will ensure a sufficient income to cover the basic expenses for workers of accommodation, food, transport and medical and childcare. It 'enables workers to live with dignity and to participate as active citizens in society.' It also strengthens families as mothers and fathers may no longer need to work two or three jobs and can spend quality time with their children. Local and overseas research indicates that communities and local businesses thrive when workers are no longer so stressed and have a small amount of discretionary spending. The yearly figure is established by independent research by the Family Centre Social Policy Research Unit.

On 18 May a FIRST Union[17] delegate spoke to the Waikato Regional Council Transport Committee about bus driver wages in the region. He expressed concern about the current wage rates for bus drivers, as some he knew had needed to use food banks. The company he works for has a starting rate of $17.25 per hour. He said their drivers have been fighting for a Living Wage for too long and a lot are considering leaving the industry. A response from the transport committee is awaited. He felt he had been heard and that people do care. Negotiations continue.

The Living Wage Movement Aotearoa New Zealand (LWM) was launched in Wellington and Auckland in 2012. Other areas followed. It has three strands of membership: people from unions, and from faith-based and community organisations. With shared values of justice and respect for all people, they work together to raise awareness of the consequences of low incomes on individuals and their communities, and to train workers in discovering their political power. Wealthy corporates and large public institutions are the prime targets of their campaigns.

This training, currently yearly in Auckland and Wellington, is led by a dynamic US Catholic nun, Sister Maribeth Larkin. She is a member of the Los Angeles Sisters of Social Service, a qualified social worker, and for the last 40 years has been employed by various local organisations in California, New York and Texas, all of which are affiliated with the Industrial Areas Foundation. She is currently working for the IAF to support organising in Australia and New Zealand, as well as in the United States. In her work in various countries, Sister Maribeth assists institutional leaders from churches, synagogues, schools and unions in learning how to develop relational power and engage in a process of practical democracy.

She teaches ordinary people how to shape and influence public policy around issues including increasing wages and benefits, health care availability and education reform, and has taught in New Zealand several times. She cites Avishai Margalit's 1996 book *The Decent Society* as a guiding light: 'The thesis is that a decent society is one whose structures do not limit people and whose citizens do not humiliate each other.' And 'We're trying to create these kinds of relationships, networks and organisations to teach people how to build bridges across race, language, religion, culture and economic status, to build trust and act together on the issues we want to work on.'

Sister Maribeth grew up in an involved parish family and Catholic Social Justice teaching made sense. She entered her order in 1970, part way through her social work studies. Sisters of Social Service, a Benedictine-based order, was founded by a remarkable Hungarian woman, Sister Margaret Slachta (1884–1974) whose mission statement was 'Go out of the desert and into the centre of life.' 'We are to be pioneers for a better world, working for social reform, not through decrees imposed by power but through renewal of the spirit from within.'

In Maribeth's early parish work she was engaged in distributing food etc to the needy but came to recognise a different calling – to empower people to bring about change in unjust structures for themselves, 'renewing the(ir) spirit from within', helping them discover the shared values and power of working on common concerns with others from different backgrounds. In other words, equipping them with the fishing rod, not simply giving a fish.

I was privileged to be part of her recent Wellington training. The social justice I learned in the Catholic context is deeply important to me. There were some key learnings from those two days with Maribeth and 28 others from various backgrounds.

There was the crucial nature of intentional relational conversations in all organisational contexts as the basis for group action – the sitting together for one-to-one conversations to establish relationship and establish common values. This is mandatory for all in leadership roles who want to maintain the energy and effectiveness of their organisation. Then the personal connecting before group meetings. The beginning point of the course was each of us introducing ourselves and our backgrounds to the group. The tangata whenua present recognised this as what they already do: acknowledging relationship before getting on with business, an important aspect of whakawhānaungatanga. This can be an unusual initial component in pākehā business meetings. Some of us came away planning to incorporate this into our organisation's systems.

It became apparent early that the training was broad-based, though offered only to members of organisations affiliated to LWM. We could apply it in any context. One exercise got the people from each of the three strands together, and we were all then to ponder our learning to critique our own institutions. And then come up with a feasible next step to improve matters. For me, writing this article is part of that.

We learned about the Organising Cycle. This is the progression:

- Listening/Relating (individuals and small groups),
- Discerning issues together and Planning,
- Acting/Negotiating, Evaluating and Celebrating – then repeat!

And about key concepts of activism, e.g. the Iron Rule (never do anything for anyone they can do for themselves), research, power analysis, negotiations.

We practised a negotiating scenario with teams of four 'employers' and 'employees' bargaining towards a Living Wage deal. A lot of learning in that one – I was very uncomfortable being a hard-nosed employer!

So we came away empowered by learning and recognising common values and passion with many different 'others'.

As background for this article I looked at the online list of Living Wage employers in New Zealand. I found Anglican, Methodist and Presbyterian parishes and organisations, but so far no Catholic ones. Are there readers – employers or employees – out there who are willing to help move this campaign along to further justice and the dignity of hard-working Kiwis?

> On 14 Sept. 2020 *The Dominion Post* reported, 'Urban bus drivers are ecstatic over a milestone living wage deal after years of protests and union fights. ... The new deal with NZTA will see bus companies continue to pay the same wages as before, with the Transport Agency making up the difference.'

Abortion – A Middle Way?

I am a woman. I am a mother. I am a feminist.

Abortion is a tortured and complex topic – and one on which parliamentarians will be voting. My comments exclude pregnancies resulting from rape, incest, in under 16-year-olds and in unusual family circumstances. As with the End of Life Choice Bill, both the 'always' and 'never' lobbies need to be heard, then a middle way found to figure a right way forward. Extreme positions serve a valuable function in a democratic society by producing arguments for the pros and the cons, each having some valid points that must somehow be integrated.

> Published as an opinion piece in *The Dominion Post*,[54] and also included in the St Andrew's parish submission to the 2019 Select Committee considering Abortion Law reform.

I went through a medically hazardous pregnancy, at the end of which both the baby and I could have ended up dead. Doctors made no promises. I had the best possible medical grounds to have an abortion. By my free choice, it was not an option for me/us. I was fortunate to have family and community support, and a confidence in the future. However, the fraught experience gave me a compassionate understanding of how it must be for pregnant women with health and other pressures who, without those resources immediately and obviously available, choose abortion. The baby and I survived, and he is now a man I am proud of.

Physical health issues in pregnancy are rarely potentially fatal. Mental health as a valid reason for abortion surely entails more than the understandable acute distress and fear about an unexpected, unwanted, inconvenient pregnancy. Maternal mental health units provide good appropriate support. But where do valid mental health concerns connect with basic if acute human distress? I shared a hospital cubicle once with a woman who said she would tell the doctors it was abortion or suicide, 'but don't worry, I don't mean it'.

As a 'thinking' as well as 'feeling' woman, prior to making important decisions, I gather all relevant information, and look at consequences of each choice and who else might be affected. As I have heard the pro-abortion discussions, there seems to be an impermeable information barrier. Suggestions that women considering abortion should see a scan before finally deciding have met with strong opposition. Scans provide pertinent information on what is happening in utero. Something there is alive, which after the abortion will be neither there nor alive.

I would want to ask myself whether it was the pregnancy, the actual birth or the 18 or so years parenting that was my key issue. Under most circumstances, the first two, difficult as they may, be can be managed with appropriate support, then parenting can be delegated by adoption. Adoptions are open these days and not the cruel affairs of the

1950s and 60s. I would weigh a hard year or two for myself against giving the foetus/baby a chance at a long and fruitful life.

As a feminist, I was outraged at reports from India that girl foetuses were being selectively aborted solely for gender reasons. All those incipient girls, incipient women denied a chance at life! It was technology-assisted genocide, another chapter in the millennia-old process of attacking women. Then I had to challenge myself on gender bias. Was I as concerned for the lives of male foetuses? They too deserve a chance at life.

As a woman, I grieved with the friend whose first grandchild was aborted, because it would have interfered with her daughter's OE. As a counsellor I met women who had thought having an abortion was fine and were then shocked by the emotional repercussions they experienced. I also was astonished the first time. On 5 November eight women spoke out about the toll this supposedly simple problem-solving procedure has taken on their lives. They were unprepared for their post-abortion emotional experiences. They called for clear information on this possibility to be included in the preparation for an abortion and the subsequent counselling. Going public with their stories was courageous, and their call should be heeded in the service of fuller information.

As with the End of Life Choice Bill, I believe legislation founded on fear and feelings is not good legislation. In both circumstances, ahead of radical interventions, there needs to be assisted rigorous analysis of the specific problems faced by individuals, and coordination of specific personal and communal solutions. Also, there should be personal commitments by women to, where possible, avoid situations that could cause unwanted pregnancies – contraception, rational analysis and personal responsibility-taking for competently managing one's own safety.

To reform the abortion legislation, let's work for a middle way. Ideally this would be where fully informed women would know what specific appropriate support is available at each stage of pregnancy should they make a free, rational and responsible choice to continue it. And in the truly extreme cases the woman's choice would be attended to with both full awareness and appropriate compassion.

Hope and Healing in Prison

God is Love! But simply telling people that is counter-productive. Love in action is what heals. Too many of our young people have been subjected to neglect and often poverty-related abuse and violence from childhood. No wonder so many self-medicate with alcohol and drugs.

> An offering of voluntary time at Arohata Women's Prison proved a very privileged and enriching experience.[55]

At Arohata Women's Prison near Wellington there is a special programme in operation. It is the Drug Treatment Programme (DTP). Groups of up to 10 women at a time are selected for the programme which lasts for three months. The times overlap – Group 1 begins in the programme as Group 2 begins the 6 weeks leading up to their graduation. During the programme, beyond the support from Corrections officers, chaplains and other staff, they have intensive therapy, and input/support from a range of volunteers. They learn yoga, quilting (and finish one or more to take home), attend Alcoholics Anonymous meetings working the 12-step programme, experience the Catholic-based grief programme Seasons for Growth, and learn public speaking skills at the fortnightly Toastmasters meeting. This is where I've recently been privileged to fit in. The three people I've joined have been offering this programme there for over eight years.

There's a wise saying about 'hearing people into speech', and this is what we do. We coach all members of the combined groups in both listening and speaking, as well as in managing formal meeting procedures. The Toastmasters' dynamics work even for the shyest and most nervous, as they do in the outside world. Lots of praise and encouragement, and perhaps a suggestion towards developing the next speech. It is a delight to see the women gaining in confidence and skills over the three months. They are always so grateful for the time we spend there, and really enjoy having a corrections officer or two with us, and they value seeing a different side to their charges.

In the speeches, usually three to five minutes long, the women may tell heart-breaking stories of horrendous sexual abuse, violence, gang affiliation and homelessness, then self-medicating with alcohol or drugs to ease the pain, leading to their offending and so to prison. Some will begin speaking in te reo with their mihi. They may give well-researched self-help speeches on topics like co-dependence and social anxiety. We hear stories of faithfully supportive families, the children they will be going home to as better mums, their hopes and plans for after release. There are the inspirational speeches, the significant talents and wisdom now freer to emerge. And sometimes hugely funny speeches have all of us laughing uproariously. Recently, letters of farewell to the drugs that had both sustained and captured them were very moving.

The culmination of their course learning comes at the six-weekly graduation ceremonies. Volunteers, staff and clinical people are welcomed onto what is their marae for the occasion by some rousing kapa haka. Wonderful energy, style and mana! Group 1 chooses one of their number to lead the occasion. This woman welcomes the manuhiri – volunteers and others – by their contribution or role, often initially in te reo, and then in what they call te reo pākehā. She addresses her own group, then those graduating. A recent speaker included these words (quoted with her permission):

> He wāhine, He wāhine toa
>
> On behalf of Group 1, we thank you for allowing us the insight and privilege of seeing your journey, for walking beside us as we began ours, for imparting all your wisdom and knowledge to each and every one of us, for all your support.

> You are all true role models and leaders, which leaves really big boots to fill!
>
> We wish you the best of luck when you leave, and courage as you further put your learning into practice.
>
> Choose to live by choice, not chance.
> Choose to be motivated, not manipulated.
> Choose to be useful, not used.
> Choose to make changes not excuses.
> Choose to excel, not compete.
> Choose self-esteem, not self-pity.
> Choose to listen to your inner voice, not to the random opinion of others.
>
> Remember knowing is not enough, for we must apply it. Wishing is not enough, for we must do!

She then calls on those graduating strong women, wāhine toa, to each give a speech. A brief introductory karakia is not unusual. Some general themes are heartfelt gratitude to Corrections officers for their respect and compassion, to therapists, and each group of volunteers; their learnings from the programme; their new self-respect, and hope and intentions for the future. They are grateful to each other for the love and nurture they have shared as a group. Every single speech is inspirational, particularly with the increased confidence that is so observable from when we first met them. Most actually look different, softer, more relaxed, and much more in touch with their own selfhood, with plans for a good clean, sober future. Boxes of tissues are supplied and frequently used both by the graduates and the visitors. They receive their certificates from the clinical people and thank them, often with big hugs.

Then others are invited to speak. The Corrections staff are impressive in the compassion that has obviously been shown within their duty of care. Volunteer representatives respond. Group 1, who are now to become Group 2 themselves, speak appreciatively of the love, guidance and nurture they have been given by the graduating Group 2 women.

To conclude, there are more waiata, including a sung version of the AA Serenity Prayer: in both te reo and English:

> God, grant me the serenity to accept the things I cannot change, the courage to change the things I can, and the wisdom to know the difference.

Then we share kai.

Each graduation ceremony has its own flavour as each group has developed its own way of being together. Transformation metaphors flow: we see tight buds opening out to beautiful flowers, formerly earthbound caterpillars stretching their wings after their chrysalis confinement, Easter resurrections out of terrible pain, new life for spirits that had been crushed into hopelessness.

In real terms, they are not all going to make it this time. A few don't make it as far as graduation before being taken off the programme. Each group usually has one or two going through for the second time. It is so crucial that when they are released there will be adequate support, accommodation, a job.... And all that soon enough for the learnings of this intensive three months course to be still accessible for them.

The good work that is being done in prisons gets very little acknowledgement. Having a glimpse of what goes on inside this unit is both a real eye-opener and a great privilege. To all staff, therapists and to the women themselves, kia kaha! The late Celia Lashlie would have nodded and said, 'Yes, I told you that prison could be the making of women, because it is often the first time that they have been safe and nurtured.'

And a plea to employers: take a chance on one of these women. They deserve, after all they have learned and all the struggle to change, opportunities not to be funnelled back into their previous destructive ways of coping with life.

It's the Love that does it! God at work in these women's lives and in the lives of all who work with them. Love from therapists, Corrections staff, volunteers and from each other, as they learn compassion for themselves and others.

Covid-19 led to the cancellation of all volunteer participation at the prison. This will hopefully resume in the near future.

Doing Racial Justice

I caught myself being surprised and immediately felt ashamed. I think both feelings were well enough concealed. I was talking to a young brown woman from a less-than-developed country and she'd just told me she was here to do a Master's degree. I'd thought I'd worked enough on my racial biases and accepted the reality of white privilege, but here was another challenge. So I knew I needed to read the book that lit up on the library shelf: *The Inner Work of Racial Justice: Healing Ourselves and Transforming Our Communities Through Mindfulness*.

> Discovering that what I'd thought I had pretty well sorted actually wasn't.

Through mindfulness and compassion practices, Rhonda Magee, an African American law professor, invites the reader to scrutinise gently their personal history of racial awareness. I have been doing that.

In the late 1940s and early 1950s in the north of England, I never saw anyone but white Caucasians. Any sense of tribalism was based on us Catholics who were Right, and The Rest who were Wrong. Earlier the Germans were the ones I'd had nightmares about, but that 'got sorted'. We saw our first people of colour in the West Indies in 1952 during the six-week voyage to New Zealand via the Panama Canal.

I was astonished, as I continued with the mindfulness exercises, to find the thought pop up, 'What about Wopsy?'[18] A hunt on my book-case revealed four 1940s books I'd read as a child in England. Wopsy was a little guardian angel who was deployed to look after a black baby in Africa with 'a white soul because he'd been baptised,' not like the other black people with black souls. I read on with mounting horror. 'God said Wopsy could call him (the baby) anything he liked because he only had a horrible pagan name…' 'The guardian angels of ordinary babies have not a very great deal to do, but of course it's rather different when the baby is a black one and a pagan one too.' '… it can't be very interesting for them (the angels) to look after a lot of pagans.' And so on, through four white-child-friendly books. And missionaries who dined on elephant steaks! It was writ large that I'd had my first lessons in racism from books approved by English Catholic bishops. I prefer to think it was the 'English' imperialism rather than the 'Catholic' that was the sad greater influence.

I'd moved on by the time I visited San Francisco in 2008, just prior to the presidential election. It was Halloween and a street party had hundreds of happy families in fancy dress. A black boy about 12 was dressed in a suit, white shirt and tie, and was being made a fuss of and recognised as 'Barack Obama' – it was lovely to see him proudly accepting the recognition. And there was an angelic little black girl with a long white dress and wings, but her whitened face broke my heart. What have we done? Why was that thought necessary?

Aotearoa New Zealand holds different memories and stories. Before we came in 1952, my parents had been told the Māoris (sic) were 'no trouble' and race relations here were just fine. Other than a couple of Māori children in my class at school and a few kuia with moko who sat smoking their pipes on the Tauranga footpath in town, we really had no contact with them.

In the 1970s, Māori voices became louder in demands for justice and the recognition of the Treaty of Waitangi. This terrified my parents: 'They just want to push us all out into the sea!' I could see the Māori perspective, but they weren't interested. I was one of the thousands who marched in the 1981 protests against the Springbok tour.

More recently I was a guest in a home where the host made a putting-down remark to a Māori visitor. I regret now that I prioritised courtesy in my role as a guest over calling him on the remark, instead of standing with the one with the least power.

Major efforts have been made here to shift the racial power balance, but Oscar- winning film-maker Taika Waititi still can say New Zealand is racist as f***.[19] A torrent of pākehā indignation, but also hopefully some interest in exploring what he means. He's been praised patronisingly for how well he has done, 'for one of his people'. My words were nothing like as explicit, but I can see now that some years ago I responded with a bit too much enthusiasm to a Pasifika woman who had just finished her law degree.

The same Taika offers a graphic lesson when in his film[20] he has little Jojo drawing the image of Jews that he's been fed. Horns, tails and all the trimmings. Gross prejudice (pre-judging) was toxic then and is still. The lesser versions in my experiences are still hurtful to those on the receiving end. I've now learned the terms micro-aggression and casual racism. Not just the blatant variety of racism hurts.

I suspect there's always more to learn about Doing Racial Justice. It isn't comfortable but learning to spot it rather earlier in myself is a step in the right direction. Compassionate Mindfulness can be a very good teacher.

That all happened three months before the tragic US police murder of George Floyd, and the subsequent demonstrations around the world supporting the Black Lives Matter and police reform campaigns. I didn't participate in the Wellington events as we were still social distancing due to Covid-19, but I was there in spirit. Here too, there has been soul-searching about racism by police and the wider community, not without complaint by some.

A Closer Look at Forgiveness

Forgiveness has been an on-going topic of interest for several years. This paper was published in *Presence*, The Spiritual Directors International Journal.[56]

I offer this reflection because as a spiritual director, counsellor, chaplain in a mental health context and former Women's Refuge educator, I have listened to many traumatised people wrestling with the subject of forgiveness, and often their guilt at being unable to do what they believe is necessary. While my case studies relate to women I have worked with, I am confident that the issues raised can also be pertinent to male spiritual directees. Many years ago, I wrestled with the topic after a life-changing experience of abuse of power. I struggled with how to forgive and guilt at being unable to do so. A therapist who called herself a non-believer yet described her practice as based on agape, told me, 'You don't have to forgive'. This sounded quite shocking at first but became powerfully freeing and healing. Then in my professional work I discovered I was far from alone in this experience, and that began this theological exploration ...

Forgiveness, like dynamite, is a potent force, and can cause problems if misused. In the Christian community and beyond, forgiveness is considered the desirable if not imperative response by someone who has been injured to the one responsible. It is almost invariably presented in Christian settings as a given, a necessary response to harm done to one's self, with an assumption that we all know what is meant by the word. This understanding is transmitted as an important component of the gospel teaching of Jesus, as a primary characteristic of the whole Christian ethos, and is often contrasted with the lack of this teaching in other faith traditions. It is how we try to avoid the cycle of revenge and bitterness that can be observed continuing for generations in some parts of the world. It is often promoted, particularly in a range of churches, as a necessary step on the route to healing from an injury, with the corollary that refusing to forgive is sinful, makes the injured party bitter and causes further harm.

I too believed whole-heartedly in the necessity of forgiveness as the appropriate response to all injury, until some personal and professional experiences provoked me to have another look. The interface between religious belief and mental health and well-being is crucially important, and I believe with Jung that all our emotional difficulties implicate our meanings and values.

A simplistic understanding of forgiveness can be actually harmful to victims in some circumstances. I also believe that whatever work spiritual directors do on their own experiences of trauma, efforts to forgive and their understanding of the issues involved, they will be better able to accompany their spiritual directees on a journey of healing.

I hope through this reflection spiritual directors may develop a more nuanced ability to be with people struggling with the topic of forgiveness, a better understanding of the process of recovery from trauma, and enhanced pastoral sensitivity. To explore the common current understanding of forgiveness in some depth and its possible outcomes, I offer case studies, scriptures and other resources for consideration. The key focus is 'What would Jesus, the Compassion of God, want for victims damaged by others?'

Common Understanding
The prevailing religious and cultural stories about forgiveness are along these lines: it is good, necessary, Christian, what Jesus said to keep doing, loving, reconciling, freeing, and – importantly – opens the way to being forgiven and healed oneself. And in contrast, unforgiveness is wrong, unloving, un-Christian, makes you bitter and vengeful, is bad for you, means you won't be forgiven your own failings. And so on.

The Teaching
The source of these perceptions is generally church teaching and scripture. Four Sunday statements I have personally heard from ministers of various denominations:

> 'Revenge …. appeals to justice. Forgiveness is about love.'

> 'Anyone who refuses to forgive has one foot in hell.'

> 'Refusal to forgive is a cancer of the soul.'

> 'Anyone who says they have forgiven but not forgotten, hasn't forgiven.'

These don't leave a hearer in any doubt about the necessity of forgiving.

And then there are the familiar Gospel texts:

> 'Yes, if you forgive others their failings, your heavenly Father will forgive you yours, but if you do not forgive others, your Father will not forgive your failings either.' (Matthew 6:14-15)

> Peter… said 'Lord, how often must I forgive my brother if he wrongs me? As many as seven times?' And Jesus answered, 'Not seven, I tell you, but seventy-seven times.' (Matthew 18:21-22)
>
> The story of the unforgiving debtor. (Matthew 18:23-35)
>
> 'When you stand in prayer, forgive whatever you have against anybody, so that your Father in heaven may also forgive your failings too'. (Mark 11:25)
>
> 'Grant pardon and you will be pardoned.' (Luke 6:37)
>
> 'If your brother does something wrong, reprove him and, if he is sorry, you must forgive him. And if he wrongs you seven times a day, and comes back to you seven times and says, 'I am sorry', you must forgive him. (Luke 17:3)
>
> 'Father, forgive them; they do not know what they are doing'. (Luke 23:34)
>
> And the Sunday-by-Sunday, even day-by-day, repetition of the Lord's Prayer: 'Forgive us our sins, as we forgive those that sin against us.'

To resist this sort of pressure takes considerable personal courage. However, there is burden enough for spiritual directees and others who are living with the effects of trauma, without having added to that the guilt at being unable to forgive and reconcile.

Real Experiences
So where does all that leave a spiritual directee – or a spiritual director – if, despite their best efforts, they find themselves unable to think, feel or say 'I forgive you' in their own understanding of those words? Perhaps spiritual directors might choose to engage with any struggles they themselves may have had around forgiving those who had caused them significant harm, their own inability to let go and reconcile with a perpetrator. The feelings may be similar to those I have both experienced myself and heard from many others: guilt and anxiety about being unable to forgive, which often become a burden that not only impedes healing, but also consumes valuable energy that would be better spent on doing that personal work.

Here are four real-life case studies from my personal and professional experience for reflection. All names are fictitious. As a spiritual director, what are your feelings on and understandings of the situations? What would you offer the spiritual directee? What supports your suggestions? How do you see God as present in each of the possibilities you might offer?

> Michelle comes to you distressed because some years ago she and her husband Jim, both Christians, forgave a relative who had sexually abused their six year-old daughter. When they confronted him, he had apologised and promised not to do it again, so they had not laid charges and continued to welcome him into their home. She has recently discovered that he had gone on to abuse many other children, fears her forgiveness facilitated the re-offending, and wonders what went wrong.

> Kate is regularly beaten by her partner but believes that if she is to receive forgiveness herself, she must continue to forgive him each time he apologises. She has left him with the support of Women's Refuge, but believes it is the Christian thing to reconcile and go back when he has apologised and promised (again) not to repeat the violence.
>
> Jane had a breakdown after a rape experience and remains severely depressed. She feels guilty that she 'can't forgive him'. Also, she misses her church community but is afraid to go back, because based on past experience she believes they will pressure her to forgive and attribute her on-going mental health problems to her 'refusal' to do so. She is receiving therapy.
>
> Nancy, an ordained priest, has resigned from all ministry because she 'can't forgive' the terrorists who killed her daughter in a bombing. She says she can no longer honestly preach forgiveness and reconciliation. Her resignation has been accepted.

What do spiritual directors make of these situations? What would Jesus do for these damaged people who, despite their best efforts, can't forgive? Where does healing lie?

Spiritual directees may have encountered what is effectively spiritual abuse. A friend who some years ago was being beaten by her husband talked about this to her minister. She was advised, 'Forgive him, go home and try harder to be a good wife'. Not at all OK! Instructions like that, assurances that 'God heals marriages', and the ministers' statements quoted earlier are what give rise to a Women's Refuge worker's rather shocking analysis of the Church generically as, 'an institutional support for battering.' I understand there is now training here for clergy on domestic violence. Hopefully this is both mandatory across denominations and ongoing. Spiritual directors are in a useful position to name this spiritual abuse and support spiritual directees in setting aside misguided advice.

When I heard her story from Jane, I wondered what Jesus would do, took a deep breath and said, 'You do not have to forgive.' I was astounded by the reaction – there was a huge physical shift from her being bowed over, to standing up straight, and saying, 'That is a huge weight off my shoulders'. Coaching in compassion for oneself and in patience for the long healing process is what truly helps. As can, with the spiritual directee's permission, a spiritual director's communication with the therapist.

And in Nancy's story, what if, instead of having her resignation from priesthood promptly accepted, she had been encouraged to be gentle with her own grief and trauma, understood with compassion, and been given leave and supportive space in which to heal? Her own capacity for ministry would undoubtedly have been significantly enriched by such an experience.

Reflections

Here are some thoughts from several years' pondering where God's healing lies for traumatised spiritual directees and other clients:

To whom was Jesus speaking to when urging forgiveness? Very likely to men who had been brought up with 'an eye for an eye and a tooth for a tooth', which itself was a development from the unrestrained revenge of earlier times. Certainly not to battered women!

When does repeated forgiveness become collusion? Some Christians find it very easy to resort to a literal understanding of the Gospel text: 'Jesus said just keep on forgiving.' We live in different days now, with different understandings of the complexities of human behaviour and the effects of trauma.

Power issues around forgiveness: the stories Jesus told were more about the powerful forgiving the less powerful, than about powerless victims forgiving powerful perpetrators.

Possible gender issues: *Communicating Forgiveness*,[21] a book on forgiveness in committed relationships, has 49 moving stories of reconciliation. When I looked more closely, there were 12 stories about men forgiving their women partners, and 37 about women forgiving their men. The happily married male authors had not noticed this disparity. My professional and personal experience leads me to think women may have greater difficulty sorting the distinctions between forgiveness, reconciliation and victimhood, and perhaps have a greater motivation towards reconciliation. Without exonerating all women or misjudging all men, statistically speaking perpetrators of abuse and violence are likelier to be male. Gender difference in the perception and practice of forgiveness is an area that deserves significant research.

What are the actual implications of the word 'forgiveness'? This gets used and preached as though we all know what we all mean: it is generally understood as letting go of anger and reconciling. What if there is a valid spectrum of possible outcomes? What might one actually do? It could range from full restoration of relationship, to letting go of anger without resuming relationship, through acknowledging the reality of what happened, to simply not choosing revenge.

What about cyclic or addictive behaviours of perpetrators? Women's Refuge workers know the part forgiveness plays in the cycle of violence, and that it is often harder for Christian women to leave abusive situations than for others. Forgiving alcoholics or drug addicts their hurtful and damaging behaviours is a pointless exercise – sanity lies in Al-Anon's 'Detach with love'. Paedophilia too is addictive – information not available to the parents of the first case study.

Can the black-white dichotomy of 'Forgiving' and 'Unforgiving' be prised apart to make a space for accountability and justice-seeking? A 2003 paper by New Zealand Psychology Professor Tony Taylor[22] described justice as a basic human need, as necessary as the other basics of life referenced in Maslow's hierarchy of needs.[23] Justice is not, as one of the clergy quoted earlier stated, equivalent to revenge. The Restorative Justice framework may have a role to play here.

I get concerned for the long-term well-being of the families of murder victims who announce that they have forgiven the killers within a day or two of the incident, often to an approving audience of fellow Christians. The normal human healing process is being short-circuited in a possibly risky way. If normal and natural emotional responses are suppressed indefinitely the outcomes can predictably be depression and physical illness.

Other perspectives
There are other reference points and other sources that I have found helpful.

Judith Herman in *Trauma and Recovery: Mourning Traumatic Loss*[24] says that survivors 'trying to bypass their outrage through a fantasy of forgiveness are attempting empowerment. But trauma is not exorcised by hatred or love.' Forcing forgiveness is likely to be impossible, so grieving the traumatic experience and focusing on healing is what is possible. Later the perpetrator may become uninteresting – but this is not forgiveness.

Community or church disapproval, whether perceived or real, of a victim's inability to forgive does not help healing. Are spiritual directors in general taught basic information about Post Traumatic Stress Disorder and the need for community support? PTSD needs to be understood as a brain injury which needs professional care. It is not amenable to the spiritual discipline of attempting forgiveness. Any spiritual directees suffering nightmares, flashbacks, hyper-vigilance, repetitive thinking or 'videos' must be referred for therapy. Spiritual direction still has a place in this journey of healing. The spiritual director can support the process by compassionate gentle care and might usefully encourage the letting go of any sense of obligation to forgive.

Kairos Document[25]
Here are some significant quotations from the *Kairos Document*, the 1985 statement by 150 South African theologians on 'forgiveness and reconciliation' versus 'prophetic action' in the efforts to end apartheid. They contrast 'standard Church Theology' with the need for a 'Prophetic Theology' where there is oppression.

> No reconciliation, no forgiveness, and no negotiations are possible without repentance (p. 12)

> There can be no real peace without justice and repentance… like Jesus, we must expose (this) false peace, confront our oppressors and sow dissension. (p. 14)

> When Jesus says we should turn the other cheek he is telling us we must not take revenge… not that we should never defend ourselves or others. (p. 15)

> ... we can point to a lack of social analysis. Church Theology tends to make use of absolute principles and apply them indiscriminately and uncritically to all situations Very little attempt is made to analyse what is actually happening in our society and why. (p. 16)
>
> Throughout the Bible, God appears as the liberator of the oppressed. He (sic) is not neutral. He does not attempt to reconcile Moses and Pharaoh, the Hebrew slaves with their oppressors... God takes sides with the oppressed. (p. 20)
>
> The Church must help people understand their rights and their duties. There must be no misunderstanding about the moral duty of all who are oppressed to resist oppression and to struggle for liberation and justice. (p. 27)

In their terms, standard Sunday Christian teaching about forgiveness and the earlier quotations are archetypal Church Theology, without the social analysis of what really happens to real people! As an aside, the response might be 'But what about the wonderful post-apartheid Truth and Reconciliation process in South Africa?' Given the on-going problems there, there is growing appreciation that this may well have taken place too early in the process, before enough healing had actually happened.

Counsellors on Forgiveness

Several years ago, I led a workshop on this topic with a group of New Zealand counsellors to discover how others in a more secular context approached this topic. They generated the following list of considerations, some of which would parallel those of many spiritual directors, and others of which are worth serious consideration:

> Our personal attitudes to and experiences with injury and forgiveness influence our approach to clients when forgiveness of an injury is an issue of theirs. This may involve whether to forgive, unwillingness to forgive, guilt at being unable to do so, and the implications of doing so or not.
>
> Belief systems must be re-examined and renegotiated to ensure they are life-giving. Forgiveness is contra-indicated if:

- It is too soon
- Anger and other feelings have been suppressed, especially when there is significant trauma
- It is under duress/pressure, seen as a moral duty
- It is part of an abuse cycle
- It is to help the perpetrator in some way (misplaced compassion)
- There are addictive behaviours involved
- When it is conditional – e.g. in the hope of restored love/acceptance

- When it is for the 'greater good' but damaging to the person
- When some institutional responsibility would be short-circuited
- When there is institutional support for the offending to continue

Forgiveness is nonetheless compatible with laying charges or complaints. This is handing over to the community responsibility for dealing with the offender and the offence.

The lived-out implications of forgiveness could range along a continuum from full re-commitment to the relationship and re-building trust, through moving on, letting go, unclipping a relationship, re-deploying energy, a deep acceptance of the reality of what has occurred to simply not seeking revenge.

Ideas for helping clients:
- Permission to not forgive.

- Encouraging them to give priority to their own feelings and process, e.g. anger, grief. Where these are suppressed any short-term relief prejudices longer term well-being.

- Alternative Bible quotations to those requiring forgiveness, e.g. the Hebrews did not have to forgive the Egyptians – they were told to get away (Exodus 3:10); God is more interested in your recovery than in your ability to forgive (Luke 4:18).

- Referral to a trained spiritual director if a counsellor is uncomfortable with a client's belief system. Consultation between a counsellor and spiritual director with the client's consent can be helpful.

- Recognition by counsellor of developmental stages of maturity and faith, e.g. Fowler's Stages of Faith.

The outcome for the person who forgives can be freedom and peace, a sense of a hold being broken, an ability to re-deploy energy, taking back one's power and strength. They alone can determine the timing.

The outcome for a person who sees themselves as withholding forgiveness can be the same.

The counsellors' conclusions are supported by another quotation from *Communicating Forgiveness*:

> Individuals who forgive too readily may be maintaining an unhealthy co-dependent relationship with a repeat offender. Low self-esteem and/or low relational power may discourage them from fully confronting wrongdoing. Forgiveness is potentially harmful because the goal is to maintain the relationship at the price of continuing unhealthy patterns of behaviour.

Are there other pertinent, more healing scriptures? Perhaps:

- Let my people go. (Exodus 5:1, Jerusalem Bible)
- He does not break the crushed reed, nor quench the wavering flame. (Isaiah 42:3, Jerusalem Bible)
- 'Get up, take the child and his mother with you and escape into Egypt...' (Matthew 2:13, Jerusalem Bible)
- 'The Spirit of the Lord is upon me... he has sent me to heal the broken-hearted, to preach deliverance to the captives... to set at liberty them that are oppressed.' (Luke 4:18, King James Version)
- 'They (the Pharisees) tie up heavy burdens, and lay them on others' shoulders...' (Matthew 23:4, Jerusalem Bible)

Importantly, the original Greek scriptural word that has been translated to English as 'forgive' is word ἀφίημί (aphiemi, Strong 863).26 It has multiple meanings: cry, forgive, forsake, lay aside, leave, let (alone, be, go, have), omit, put, send away, remit, suffer, yield up. Nothing about reconciliation! The 'let be', 'let go', 'lay aside' variations may seem like eventual healthy possibilities to damaged ones.

A map

I now hypothesise a dividing line between those victims of injury or damage whose selfhood is relatively intact after the offending, and those whose selfhood has been seriously damaged (then or previously) for the possibly long-term future. The first group's personal power may be dented by the offending, but not seriously affected. For them, generously extending forgiveness could eventually be a possible, useful and gracious gift. But the damaged psyches of the second group will need long, patient and compassionate support and therapy, and some consistent experience of living free from fear to arrive at anything like the liberation and healing promised by Jesus. They can be usefully relieved of the often guilt-inducing burden of struggling unsuccessfully to forgive. This is where a spiritual director can offer another perspective. The healing route for those 'below the line' is different from that prescribed for those 'above it'. There is a parallel here with quantum physics, where below a certain size particle, a whole different set of rules of behaviour operates, challenging the rules and systems of 'normal' physics.

Conclusion

A similar analysis of forgiveness and the care needed when working with victims of abuse is found in the writings of two Catholic clergy prominent in the support of victims of sexual abuse by clergy, Australian Bishop Geoffrey Robinson[27] and US priest Thomas Doyle. Doyle describes pressure on victims to forgive from church quarters as re-victimisation.[28] They both have a profound concern for the healing the damage done by trauma to people's spiritual journeys and recognise this can be impeded by standard simplistic understandings of forgiveness.

Given all this, I see a real need for in-depth teaching on the topic of forgiveness in any spiritual direction training course. The usually simplistic church teaching on this topic does not generally engage with social analysis and psychological realities in a way that is helpful to struggling victims of various types of abuse or betrayal. Hopefully any deeper reflection on forgiveness will better equip spiritual directors for promoting healing both for themselves, and for their spiritual directees.

The questions 'What would the loving, compassionate Holy One want for this person?' and 'What will actually promote healing?' are keys to creating a safe, healing space for damaged spiritual directees, so that they are more able eventually to move past the pain and find the wholeness, freedom and joy that is their human spiritual birthright.

Love and Parish

Love and Parish

While holding my post-denominational identity, since 2012 I have belonged to St Andrew's on The Terrace, a Progressive Presbyterian parish. Here are some of my contributions to liturgical life at St Andrew's on The Terrace. These were mostly offered to the Sunday congregations with a small group of women who had previously been together in ExAlt, a feminist group who explored women's spirituality and theology from the early 1990s, based at an Anglican parish. In 1999 we were asked to leave as we 'weren't Christian enough'. Over time, we each found our way to St A's, as we realised its theology and ethos connected with ours. Inclusive and down-to-earth language and imagery, women's ministry fully accepted, and Social Justice practised internally all contributed to the good match for us. No orthodoxy is required. There is wide range of theologies – a strong non-theist strand alongside a developing contemplative one, and others. Each Sunday bulletin invites:

> 'Whatever you believe, whatever you do not believe,
> you are welcome here.'

Diversity in its many dimensions is a key value.

Ordination

In 1994 a Catholic friend wrote a sociology research paper called *Sub-Ordination, A Study of Catholic Women's Preparedness for Ordination to Priestly Ministry*. I was one of the sample of six women interviewed. All of us felt called to ministry and were doing continuing theological and pastoral study. We were all already in various ways committed to being ministers of the Gospel in chaplaincies and pastoral work. The overall conclusion of the study was that if suddenly we'd been offered ordination to the Catholic priesthood, most of us would decline, until there was significant reform of other aspects of the church. But that scenario was never a possibility. It still isn't. In our various ways and contexts, we have ministered on. For me this has been mostly as a chaplain in workplaces, hospice and a mental health setting, and as a spiritual director. I have claimed what the Anglicans call the ordination of baptism and am comfortable with my own understanding of my ministry.

> St Andrew's on The Terrace was celebrating the 50th anniversary of the ordination of women in the Presbyterian Church. I was invited to speak about my call to ministry

Here's a poem by Edwina Gateley, another Catholic lay woman who claims her own priesthood. Oddly, as little girls we attended the same school in the 1940s in Lancaster, England.

The Anointing

There were no crowds at my ordination
– the church was cold and bare
No bishop to bless and consecrate – no organ music filled the air.
No procession went before me, no cross or incense smell
No songs or incantations, no triumphant pealing bell.
But I'd heard the children playing in the stench of city slums
And heard people sobbing at the roaring of the guns
And the stones cried out before me as the sirens wailed and roared
And blood of women and children on arid earth was poured.

There were no crowds at my ordination
– the church was cold and bare
But cries of the people gathered, and birdsong filled the air
The wind blew cold before me, the mountains rose and split
Earth shuddered and trembled, an eternal flame was lit.

> There were no crowds at my ordination
> – the church was cold and bare
> But Spirit breathed so gently in the free and open air.
> She slipped through walls and barriers
> And from stones and earth proclaimed
> Oh see, my dear, dear people
> See Woman, whom I have ordained.

It was a joy to be given acceptance in roles at St Andrew's that are normal here but simply couldn't have happened in my other life. So it's a privilege to be here, and celebrating with a church family who 'got it' half a century ago and ordained the first of their many wonderful women ministers.

New Wineskins: Progressive Christianity [29]

> A re-thinking of Christian priorities – the 8 Points of Progressive Christianity articulate principles and allow for multiple interpretations.

The term Progressive Christianity was first used in my hearing a few years ago by an Anglican priest. It was in a Catholic-sponsored context, and it provoked some discomfort. This was noticed and the words were quietly withdrawn.

It piqued my curiosity, and since then I've discovered that Progressive Christianity is a significant movement among Protestant denominations that now has an international network. It has a trans-denominational ethos and recently there have been Progressive Christianity conferences in Aotearoa New Zealand, and in Australia.

There are many thinking people in the Christian communities of Aotearoa New Zealand who would assent to the propositions of this movement. There are a number of tenets that any Gospel-centred community would recognise as valid. It might be encouraging to know there are faith communities here and round the world where these principles are officially enshrined as the working document, the mission statement, the modus operandi of involved parishes.

The difference from 'standard' Christianity lies in the ranking of priorities. Progressive Christianity's top priority is the radical inclusiveness that Jesus lived. All are welcome, unconditionally, to the community, to the table, both metaphorically and eucharistically. Those who, despite the (sometimes) preached care for them, have been marginalised by main-line churches are welcomed and valued. Gay, lesbian, bisexual, transgender and intersex people, the mentally disabled or ill, women, the divorced are all affirmed. 'All are welcome at this table', and in ministry. In the words of a familiar hymn, 'Come as you are, that's how I want you…' There are no beliefs, orthodoxies or acceptances of authority that are required for welcome into these communities. Diversity of belief and spiritual understanding is normal and respected. Such inclusivity has potential to make those of a more conservative persuasion feel uncomfortable. Some of their core beliefs about who is 'in' and 'out' are challenged.

There is acknowledgement that following the radical Gospel Jesus is counter-cultural and often not compatible with the status quo, be that religious or cultural. So there is social and structural analysis, peace work and social justice. These passions are of course common to many in many denominations. What seems different is the energy put into walking the talk, to modelling this internally within a parish, and in all the administrative practices. Huge effort is put into doing so. This is reflected in liturgy, language, theology and structures. 'Power for' rather than 'power over' is the ethos. Undoubtedly this can take longer and sometimes be messier, but outcomes are better for all involved. There is a concerted effort to encourage ministry gifts and skills among lay people.

There is an insistence on intellectual integrity, the rigorous examining of Christian assumptions, teachings, and traditions in the light of context and current knowledge. The words used in Sunday worship are congruent with the theology: the Holy is compassionate and beyond gender; immanence (panentheism – the Divine presence in and through all that is) is emphasised over transcendence, and transcendence is found in the depths of immanence; we are co-workers with the Divine, focusing on the 'salvation' of the here and now, rather than any addressing of an 'out-there-somewhere' Father/Lord, and working towards an after-life in heaven.

Atonement theology, a cornerstone of Christian orthodoxy, has been abandoned. It has been understood and preached as 'God the Father sent His Son Jesus to die for our sins.' But this understanding of the historical crucifixion of Jesus was generated in a society where the ancient tradition of blood sacrifices was still practised with animals in religious ritual. It is not compatible with the 21st century belief in a God of compassion and with Jesus' teaching on non-violence. How much more sense to acknowledge that any prophetic standing up for truth and justice against powers-that-be can be costly. It happened to the prophets, it happened to Jesus and it happens still.

It is overtly acknowledged that Christianity, Religion and Science are allies in the search for Truth. Scientific truth, the discoveries about life here and the depths of the cosmos, contribute to the development of religious thinking. With this goes commitment to the well-being of the planet and particular ecological concerns.

The validity of other faith traditions is acknowledged, along with significant commitment to interfaith work and dialogue. Christianity can value itself and its traditions even while letting go the claims to be the only Way.

Marcus Borg in *The Heart of Christianity* speaks of the differences between the 'earlier' and the 'emerging' paradigms of Christianity. They include a shift in focus from the literal-factual interpretation of the Bible, to the historical and metaphorical while acknowledging its role as 'mediating the sacred.' The overarching themes of justice, compassion, peace and equality are prioritised over literal understandings of particular texts. And the emphasis on 'salvation' has shifted from being about post-death heaven and hell, to being about 'transformation in this life through relationship with God'.

Here indeed is the new wine which has been bubbling into the spiritual life of so many faith-filled people in many denominations in recent times. For its fullest development it needs new wineskins, new structures where these understandings can be articulated, lived, shared, and modelled in an open, intentional and integrated way. This is Progressive Christianity – an opportunity to speak and worship communally as we now believe.

Mysticism and Progressive Christianity

Contemplative spirituality is an easier term than mysticism, as it focuses on the process rather than the possible product. Firstly – I am not an expert.

We're all different, so we will each relate to or connect with the Divine/God/the Sacred in our own unique way. I want to look at mysticism and specifically Christian mysticism or contemplative spirituality in the widest possible context.

> St Andrew's has a series of winter meals and talks, known as Spirited Conversations. I was surprised to be asked, and happy to offer this.

We know science has drastically reduced the number of those Earth processes which were long ago attributed to the activities of the gods, then to God. But since the dawn of human prehistory there have been those who have had experiences and tapped into wisdom, gifts and powers beyond the everyday human norm. Many indigenous peoples still have their shamans, medicine people. In European history, the Celts and others had their wise women, the healers and knowers, those with 'the gift'. It makes sense to me that this human shamanic gift has continued down the ages. Human brains are wired differently from each other, and some seem to be wired for a particular sensitivity that transcends the time/space dimension. There may be a genetic component to this.

I believe that Jesus, whoever and whatever else he may be, was firmly in this shamanic tradition, which is why I personally have no problem believing the miracle stories. Western scientists in the 21st century are discovering more about the powerful effects of meditation and the human brain. Jesus taught his way of truth, justice and love, promised to send his Spirit to guide disciples into all truth, and pointed to a Way of life transformation. This Way includes whole-hearted commitment, prayer, self-discipline, service and love. 'If you love me, keep my commandments.' 'Seek first the kin-dom of

God, then all else will be added.' Francis of Assisi, with his connection to the natural world, was in the same shamanic tradition.

In the family tree of religions, shamanism came first. In the present-day Shamanic tradition, their terminology is different, but the experiences and their fruits are often very similar to those of our prayer traditions. They talk of spirit guides – and that is exactly the role Jesus holds for the Christian: teacher, guide, and maybe intermediary. For many, he is someone to spend time with, to seek help from. And shamans speak of power animals. While at first this seemed very different from any Christian thinking, eventually I've understood the concept as another set of metaphors for what we might call guardian angels. Images/imaginings of God as mother eagle and mother bear, or Jesus comparing himself to a mother hen are straight from Scripture – we just haven't called them power animals! Christian priesthood and ordained ministry are at a deep level about mediating this connection with the spiritual world, knowledge and healing.

Other faiths have their mystical traditions and very similar spiritual disciplines.

Hinduism goes back to about 5000 BCE. The common theme of their ancient text Upanishads is the merging of the individual self (Atman) with the universal source (Brahman), through active contemplation, purity of heart and the simple grace of God to aim at dissolution into the all-pervading consciousness.

Buddhism evolved from Hinduism. They teach the Noble Eightfold path to nirvana, the underlying, all-pervading consciousness: right understanding, right intention, right speech, right action, right livelihood, right effort, right mindfulness, right concentration.

The mystical Jewish tradition is the Kabbalah – universal wisdom traced back to 5000 BCE and a medieval text called Zohar. One current version of their disciplines: sharing, awareness and balance of the ego, existence of spiritual laws, we are all one, leaving our comfort zone can create miracles.

The Sufi way grew within Islam. Sufi stages of spiritual growth are repentance, surrender, voluntary poverty, patience, acceptance, gratitude, then the dark night of the soul, a place of emptiness and despair. Without any sign of hope, the soul labours on, inspired only by faith in the divine mystery – and finally experiences the revelation of Love.

These practices are all congruent with Progressive Christianity's first Point: Following the Way of Jesus.

Those great Christian mystics who have gone before us have left their writings about Love, given and received, about seeking an ever-deeper relationship with the Divine, or God, or Jesus, however we are personally drawn. It is about responding to the Divine Lure,[30] yearning for connectedness and getting glimpses of what might be. The traditional spiritual disciplines are preparation of the soul-ground, but any experiences and healing that may arise are total gifts. Prayer, meditation, symbol, image, music, ritual, art and poetry are all gateways to the experience of transcendence or immanence. Traditional sign-posts are 'pray as you can', and 'the desire to pray is a prayer itself'.

The further discipline is to stay focused on seeking the Giver rather than the gifts, not seeking for more experiences. It is also a profound journey of self-awareness towards self-transcendence with ever-greater inner healing and the consequent ability to love more deeply and sensitively: to love humans including ourselves, creatures, the earth, the cosmos. Far from being self-indulgent, this spiritual process is a significant contribution to world peace.

Shamans and other mystics often come into their power after a severe illness or trauma. Robert Grant in *Spirituality and Trauma* says: '… for people affected by trauma the meaning of life is questioned. Old answers no longer suffice. Priorities are re-ordered, concerns about identity, the value of suffering, the importance of justice and the appropriate forgiveness are big issues. … Trauma throws victims onto a path that mystics, shamans, mythic heroes and spiritual seekers have been walking for thousands of years.'

Some choose the shamanic path, others have it thrust upon them. In the Christian mystical tradition, unbroken since the earliest days, many of the saints had this experience. Julian of Norwich, the English anchorite, Hildegard, the German abbess, scientist and composer, Ignatius who founded the Jesuits, Teresa of Avila. They 'came back' from dark experiences and told us what they had experienced and learned in that other realm. It was their gift to the wider church and community.

The mystical tradition has continued: in the last 100 years there have been Evelyn Underhill, Caryl Houselander, Thomas Merton, Teilhard de Chardin, Catherine de Hueck Doherty. Currently Cynthia Bourgeault, Thomas Keating, Matthew Fox and others write to offer guidance to seekers. It is well-known that you can take people no deeper than you have been yourself.

I want to pay a tribute to my former Catholic church which, despite its many failings, preserves at its heart the tradition of spiritual growth in the contemplative way through prayer, spiritual direction and retreats. When the time was right, other denominations asked to share these treasures. In the 1980s, a Presbyterian initiative in New Zealand led to the founding of the trans-denominational Spiritual Growth Ministries which offers retreats, spiritual direction opportunities and training in the spiritual direction ministry.

So, many spiritual paths converge. Not all contemplatives or mystics live under the umbrella of religion. Those whose lives are wholly dedicated to another pursuit, e.g. music, the environment, and even it seems, dressage, also experience the moments of transcendence and immanence. Those who engage with Spirit, Life and Earth, and seek the good of all with appropriate disciplines and practices are truly pilgrim companions on the Way. We are all called to be mystics![31] Different traditions hand on the same essential wisdom – Seek! Look! Listen! Then eventually the seeking stops and the recognition arrives of what has been there all along – All is One!

There's a growing understanding among Christian people of faith that the Divine Presence is at work in and through all that is, and there is an essential unity, a real connectedness of All That Is: panentheism – 'God in everything'. Not pantheism, the more limiting 'God is everything'. This pervading Presence is the perspective that many Eastern and indigenous faiths never lost. The ancient symbol of the net of Indra is a beautiful image for this connectedness – All-That-Is as one net with, at each intersection, a multifaceted jewel which reflects everything else. Everything is present everywhere.

The same concept is supported by the newer Western scientific perspective. I've recently come across words from the quantum physicist David Bohm who writes of the world – and us, and everything – as being holograms, each fragment containing everything. Despite the limited small picture information provided to us in daily life by our senses and ordinary experience, there is this bigger picture of unity whose existence can now be discerned scientifically. What if this understanding is simply another way to describe the Mystery we call the Divine? The convergence of scientific and spiritual realities and language? The scientific discovery of the physical manifestation of the spiritual reality we have already known?

There are treasures to be discovered in following the path of seeking union with the Holy. But this seeking must be simply for the sake of the ultimate relationship, not for any gifts along the way. From my very lay reading of quantum science, light can be wave or particle, photons can be matter or energy. If the building blocks of the physical world can react ambiguously to circumstances, then it makes sense that the Divine can be sensed variously both as transcendent Life-Force in the material world, and as immanent personal loving presence. So to conclude, I see the theological and the contemplative traditions of Christianity as like the double helix of DNA. They are inseparable, and either without the other is unable to sustain a full ongoing life of the Spirit.

A New Liturgical Season: Celebrating the Season of Creation

This reflection and description of our service was written for the Catholic theology book Living in the Planet Earth: Faith Communities and Ecology *(2016).*

'Land is kept in existence by the spiritual attention of the people', said the old Indigenous man I met some years ago in Central Australia. Shaping a Sunday service has been a way to offer a parish community the opportunity to pay such deep attention to Land.

As well as Christmas and Easter-related and Pentecost liturgical seasons, several denominations in a few countries now celebrate the Season of Creation.[32] This is the four Sundays preceding the feast of St Francis of Assisi which falls on the 4th of October, so usually the four Sundays in September. It is fitting to honour St Francis in this way as his *Canticle of the Sun*[33] is one of the most well-known Christian writings honouring the environment. He praised God for Brothers Sun, Wind and Fire, Sisters Moon and Water, and Sister Mother Earth 'which sustains and keeps us' and produces fruits and flowers. There are, too, the familiar stories of Francis preaching to the birds and converting the wolf. A real Saint of the Environment.

History

This Season of Creation, an innovation in the traditional liturgical year, was initiated by Rev Norman Habel, an Australian Lutheran eco-theologian and chief editor of the Earth Bible Project.[34] There were theological considerations beside his own life-long love of the natural environment, such as that while the Christmas and Easter seasons are focused on Jesus, and Pentecost on the Holy Spirit, there could also appropriately be an annual time to focus on the Creator and Creation with gratitude, awe and repentance for the damage done to the planet Earth.

The first Season of Creation was celebrated in St Stephen's Lutheran Church, Adelaide in 2000. Between 2001 and 2005 the concept was developed through workshops and resource planning in conjunction with the Uniting Church's Commission for Mission in Melbourne. Since then, it has also been an option for parishes in New Zealand, North America and Europe. There is now a three-yearly cycle of topics and readings, with available hymns and readings. A resource for Catholic participation in the Season of Creation has been developed by the Australian Columban Missionaries.[35] This can be sent electronically to Catholic and other parishes. Parts of it can be adapted to local needs. In the 15 years since the initial celebration of the Season of Creation, the need for repentance and conversion to simpler lifestyles has intensified as the effects of climate change become increasingly evident.

A faith community celebration

St Andrew's on The Terrace in Wellington, a Progressive Presbyterian parish, has been celebrating this Season for several years, and in 2014 the nominated themes for the four Sundays in September were Rivers, Land, Forest and Wilderness. On Rivers Sunday, two parishioners, Wendy and Andrew Matthews, led the service and spoke of the rivers in their lives and experience, both personal and professional. For Forest Sunday, Kevin Hackwell, of Royal Forest and Bird Protection Society, was invited to speak, and outlined their vision for a predator-free New Zealand. On Wilderness Sunday, Rev Dr Jim Cunningham, the interim minister of the parish, explored Wilderness in geographical, metaphorical and theological terms. Along with three friends, it was my privilege to shape and lead the service for Land Sunday, and we offer here our own contributions to that service. The others each spoke on an aspect of Land, and my contribution was the formal prayers.[36] There is freedom at St Andrew's for parishioners to lead Sunday services, to develop a service form and choose readings to suit their theme of the day. Inclusive language is the norm. Full orders of service for this and all

Sunday services, including words of hymns, are online, usually along with an audio recording of the Reflection.[37]

The Land Sunday service

For the cover of our printed order of service, we used an unusual aerial photo of Wellington,[38] taken looking north from above Zealandia (formerly the Karori Sanctuary). This shows the extent of this mainland island of regenerating forest and bird sanctuary in the foreground, the city, harbour and Hutt Valley further north and in the far distance Cook Strait and Kapiti Island. There is a clear view of the Wellington Fault, running through Zealandia and along the harbour coastline. This is our particular land environment in all its beauty and fragility.

We prayed:

> We come together in the presence of the Holy One
> To honour Mother Earth, Papatūānuku and all she supports;
> To acknowledge our utter dependence on her well-being;
> And to ponder our place in the web of life.
> From her we come and to her we return.
> We honour the Land of our Earth
> In the Creative Presence we name God.

Entrance hymn: Come to our land, come to our hearts, Spirit of truth…[39]

And then as responsorial psalm:

> Fire-filled rock orbiting a star
> Deluged with stardust
> Wet, green, growing, expanding
> Life appearing
> Learning to breathe
> **– Your history is our history.**
>
> Gondawanaland
> Gaia Papatūānuku
> Maui's canoe and fish
> Body of God
> Aotearoa New Zealand
> **– Your stories are our stories.**
>
> Land for forest and food
> Māori first-comers
> Missionaries and colonisers
> Immigrants from many lands
> Peace and justice still elusive
> But perhaps some healing
> **– Your well-being is our well-being.**

Land of inner fire
Land that shakes and re-forms
Mountains, plains and coasts
Ground of our being
Source of our food
Land that loves and supports us
**– Your life is our life.
Sacred gift of Land, we bless you and honour you.**

The Gospel chosen was Matthew 25:35-40, ('Whatsoever you do to the least…') with the preamble: As we hear this familiar story, let us be aware of situations where our planet, our land and the other species in the Earth family have been hungry, thirsty, denuded, sickened, and imprisoned. The first Contemporary Reading was part of Chief Seattle's famous 1854 speech about the need to teach our children reverence for the Earth, because:

> 'Whatever befalls the earth befalls human dwellers on the earth' and whatever we do to the web of life we do to ourselves'.

The second was a question asked by Te Whiti of the land purchasing agent at Parihaka in 1879:

> 'My blanket is mine. Think you it would be right for you to try to drag it from my body, and clothe yourself with it? If I attempted to tear your coat from your back, you would resist and would not be to blame … I do not go on your land disturbing you … why do you interfere with me in the occupation of mine?'[40]

Hymn: These hills where the hawk flies lonely… [41]

There were three seven-minute reflections on different aspects of Land, summarised here by the speakers:

Sonia Groes-Petrie, a soil scientist, spoke about ways farmers are being encouraged to adopt sustainable methods of managing their land.

> I have been working over the past year for a start-up company called Regen. We create easy-to-use tools such as daily text messages and apps on mobile phones to enable dairy farmers to make informed decisions in managing their land. Our first service was a daily text alert indicating the optimal time to spray effluent on paddocks (effluent is the mix of water, cow urine and dung from the dairy shed following milking). We have sensors on the farm constantly recording soil temperature and moisture levels. This information is used to create a recommendation to the farmer on whether to irrigate the effluent today or not. Farmers are recognising that what was sometimes previously regarded as a nuisance and 'waste', is actually a wonderful resource of nutrients for the land if used wisely … A[nother] farm … is part

of Ngāti Tūwharetoa and Te Arawa's ancestral lands, the tribes to which the trust is affiliated. Māori values, such as kaitiakitanga, ensuring people and natural resources are nurtured, are critical to the success of their business. The trust has retired lands, protected wetlands and waterways, established forestry blocks, irrigates land with waste water from a Taupo wood mill and is now investing in low-impact effluent systems. They have been using the daily effluent management tool since early last year.

Sonia concluded with a Bruce Sanguin quotation:

> This is a season to regard all creation as a radiant manifestation of Spirit, and to understand that the one we call the Christ is cosmic in scope and in love. All of creation lives and moves and has its being within the heart of Christ. Our vocation is to fall back in love with creation and to treat the planet, her bio-systems, and creatures, as we treat our family.[42]

Patricia Booth spoke about Covenant, drawing connections between the Hebrew Scripture stories of covenant between God and people, and 21st century legislation in Aotearoa New Zealand which facilitates the preservation of a particular environment in perpetuity.

> In Genesis 6:18, before the Flood, God makes a covenant with Noah that Noah and all living creatures with him in the ark, will survive. Then, in Genesis 8:22, after the Flood, God says: 'While the earth lasts, seedtime and harvest, cold and heat, summer and winter, day and night, shall never cease.' Then in Genesis 9:13, the rainbow becomes 'a sign of the covenant between [God] and the earth.' Later in Isaiah 54:10 is the tremendous inspiring passage: 'Though the mountains move and the hills shake, God's love shall be immovable and never fail, and God's covenant of peace shall not be shaken.' So that is the covenant promise of the Hebrew Testament.

> Now turning to 21st century Aotearoa New Zealand, the relevant legislation is the Queen Elizabeth II National Trust Act 1977. This provides for 'open space covenants', legally binding protection agreements registered on the title of the land. The covenant binds the current AND ALL subsequent land owners. The Trust helps them legally protect special natural and cultural features on their land such as wetlands and areas of native bush, and acts as a 'perpetual trustee'. Its Mission Statement states that it aims, 'To partner with land owners to protect special places on private land for the benefit of present and future generations'.

> As at 30 June 2014, there are more than 4,300 covenants on 180,000 hectares of protected open space. Just as God's covenants as recorded in the Bible last forever, so under New Zealand legislation covenants on the land last forever. I believe these concepts of guardianship and protection of the land help us to understand and acknowledge that the land is a living

being, and therefore needs to be kept healthy – spiritually healthy as well as physically healthy.

Margaret Megwyn's theme was Legacy:

> We come from stardust. Our earth, land, sea and all living things are made of the same elements as the stars, planets, galaxies and the whole cosmos. The old idea of humans being a creation set apart has been shattered by our knowledge of evolution. Yet we know the 'dominion over' attitude still dominates.
>
> Here in New Zealand our ancestors, or parents or we ourselves have come from somewhere else, by waka, ship or plane. In spite of legal documents, we do not own the land. We have the use of the land. We put down roots and have a spiritual connection. We are guardians. I love the Māori identification with a mountain, river and place. This gives a profound sense of belonging. In 1840, the Treaty of Waitangi, with its different meanings in Māori and English, resulted in misunderstandings about sovereignty and the rights to tribal land. Subsequent confiscation of land and disregard of agreements has resulted in years of striving for justice to honour the treaty. It is important to remember that other indigenous people did not have a treaty.

Linked with this, is the uprooting of people from their place, for example, Māori in New Zealand (we think of Parihaka), Indigenous Australians, Native American and First Nation in North America. Highland Scots were pushed off their clan lands and sent overseas. The Irish were sent west or overseas. Every day the news tells us uprooting continues.

Climate change is a reality even if some politicians deny it. Low lying islands in the Pacific are being inundated by the sea. We may feel we are 'a voice crying in the wilderness' but as well as being a faith community, we are a hope community, and this is important.

Margaret shared a creed she had written many years ago:

> We pledge allegiance to Mother Earth, Papatūānuku and all she supports.
> We honour her form and diversity.
> Let her be one planet indivisible with safe air, water and soil.
> May she have economic justice and peace for all.

After these reflections, we played a recording of Chris Skinner's 'God of our island home', during which a group led by Margaret did a meditative circle dance which flowed tidally in and out around the central table.

The Prayer over the Offerings:

> We are part of the earth, sharing with all life both riches and needs.
> As we acknowledge our place in this web of life,
> And the constant interdependent flow of energy,
> May our giving contribute to ease the needs of others,
> And may our own needs be eased by the gifts of others, and our willingness to receive.

The Call to Service was based on a Joanna Macy reflection:

> Are we willing to commit ourselves daily to the healing of our world and the welfare of all being?
> To live on earth more lightly and less violently in the food, products and energy we consume?
> To draw strength and guidance from the living earth, the ancestors, the future generations and all our sisters and brothers of all species?
> To support each other in our work for the world and ask for help when we need it? To pursue a daily practice that clarifies our minds, strengthens our hearts, and supports us in our commitment?

Final Hymn: Where mountains rise to open skies, your name, O God, is echoed far… [43]

The Blessing, spoken by all:

> We bless and encourage each other
> To do Creative Spirit's work in our land
> In large ways and small,
> To move God's evolutionary process forward,
> As we cherish with gratitude
> Our whole planet, our own land
> All life, and each other.

In this Season of Creation service, we articulated our theology of Land within cosmic, mythic, historical, scientific and practical themes, and moved with our community from awe and gratitude to the opportunity for individual repentance and commitment to care for Land. We brought the new Creation Story into our liturgy to join some of the oldest Christian traditions, and together we paid deep spiritual attention to many facets of God's gift of Land.

Conclusion

This service was simply a part of the continued ecological commitment of St Andrew's people. While there is no specific environmental group, many parishioners are involved in care for the Earth as either professionals or volunteers, for example, at Zealandia. In 2015, the themes of the services were Planet, Humanity, Flora and Mountain. During September, 40 parishioners gathered to hear Dr Andrew Matthews, an international climate-change negotiator, speak on the realities we face. In the weekly bulletin parishioners were encouraged to explore their own carbon footprints, and there was a notice for a four-session climate-change course elsewhere. As a parish pilgrimage, we visited Graham and Patricia Booth's off-grid eco-home and wetland restoration in Otaki and heard of the spiritual basis of their project. And a new Season of Creation banner project was underway, to be completed by September 2016. We continue this sacred journey, individually and communally deeply grounded in our panentheism – the awareness that God is dynamically present and active in and through All That Is.

Storm Reflection

> For a later Season of Creation, I was entrusted with coordinating the Storm-themed service. Here are the Reflection and a prayer.

Thankfully, we no longer see storms as God's punishment as in the stories of Noah, Jonah and others. But we know now that storms are increasing in frequency and violence because of what has been done to the earth. We too are called to repentance and mending our ways in our care of the earth.

Storms can remain powerful and occasionally frightening experiences even with the foresight of good meteorological services. We here in Aotearoa, maybe more than some, can understand deeply the use of storm as a metaphor for the personal upheavals, tragedies and emotional disturbances of our lives. The inner thunder, the lightning strikes, the battering gales, power outages, the torrential rains that can swamp our being, rip the roofs off our previously fairly manageable lives, and cause unwelcome leaks of memories. Surrendering to the process is all that is possible. Where do we turn then for survival? Who can be the Jesus figures in our boat with us? Family, friends, neighbours do what they can to manifest Divine Presence and compassion. Therapists and medication can touch the deeper places in need of healing. Asking for support as the disciples did on the stormy lake is pretty difficult for most adults. Learning to do so is actually a spiritual maturing, as well as being a community strengthener.

As we work our way to the still core of our being, the hope offered by faith and experience that this storm too will pass can keep us from despair. External situations, or internal ones for that matter, may not be fully resolved, there may be a long wait, but, somehow, we can eventually discover a peace that we did not know was possible.

For those who follow the Way of Jesus, there is his gift of a map. In his book *Resurrecting Jesus*, Adyashanti, a Buddhist teacher, says the essence of Jesus's teaching is that the full sweep of his life, death and resurrection is the map, the model of the human spiritual journey. We all, one way or another, develop through hidden child-life, an adult sense of purpose and mission, temptations in deserts, successes, radical failures, then some new life.

If we see the final days of Jesus as a storm, there were the gathering clouds of the authorities' determination to kill him, the chill winds of the desertion by his friends, the hurricane of the agony in the Gethsemane, his ultimate choice to surrender to the force of the chaos rather than attempting to control it, the desolation and loneliness, the sheer pain of it all until it was over. We all have our own Good Fridays.

But that was not the end. Whether or not there was a literal Resurrection is less important than that Jesus emerged changed from his obliterating storm, with a new way of being in the world and of relating to the ones he loved. As the Compassion of God, he is with us in our storms, calling us on with the promise that our own gigantic waves will be stilled, our own storms will subside, our rainbows eventually appear, and so we come to our own resurrections. We too are changed by our storms. Life is different afterwards as a new normal unfolds. As in Genesis, so still now Spirit hovers over chaos in astonishing and creative ways, and we are able to find our resilience and go on.

Before his great storm hit, Jesus said, 'My peace I leave with you. My own peace I give you, a peace the world cannot give, this is my gift to you.' And afterwards as he came to his terrified disciples, again, 'Peace be with you.' So after our own storms, we too come to rainbows and peace, and eventually gratitude for what still is, for what is new, and for wisdom gained that we'd not previously needed. Peace be with us all!

Storm Prayer

When we ponder storms, so many images spring to mind:
It is easy to understand Divine Presence
in the summer storm bringing rains
that break the drought, refreshing all that grows
relieving tension and humidity.
We give thanks for life-giving waters.

We search for the God of Justice and Compassion
when storms of human-generated crisis,
involving family, community, nation or all of us
swirl around and catch us in their chaos.
**Compassionate Spirit, give us courage to row against wild tides
and clear sight to choose the right way forward.**

How do we find God when weather systems hit,
and nature's destructive overwhelming forces
against which humans are powerless
cause death and damage on land and at sea?
**Compassionate Spirit, be with us to guide, strengthen
and comfort in the storms of life.**

How do we find God in our inner storms,
when visibility is nil, our charts and compass lost,
the sand-banks moved, the beacons gone,
and sense of direction disappears?
**Compassionate Spirit, be with us to guide, strengthen
and comfort in the storms of life.**

Humanity Reflection

Look for a moment at the skin on your hands and ponder how it is the merging place of two worlds. Beyond it is the expanding world of cosmos, stars, our beautiful hurting planet and all its other inhabitants. As individuals and as a species we are an integral part of this web. Within our skin is another stardust universe of comparable complexity. Blood, bone and muscle, cells, genes, DNA, the amazing balance that at best holds us in life and health, the neuroplasticity that can re-route damaged brain functions. And within too are the immeasurable mysteries of Spirit, consciousness, awe, love, language, emotions, imagination, creativity, our facility with symbols and metaphors and so much more. As human beings, we hold this astonishing role of knowing the complexity of it all, our connectedness, and having the responsibility of responding to this awareness for our own human well-being, that of all creatures and of our planet.

> For another Season of Creation theme, Humanity, we had a patchwork service of several people's contributions. This was mine.

We here have this privilege of conscious awareness because our physical survival needs are more or less met, so our energy has been freed to reflect, research, learn and grow. As cosmologist Brian Swimme says, 'We are the Universe becoming conscious of itself.' With this privilege comes responsibility.

Swimme, in a ground-breaking set of DVDs, names and describes ten discernible processes or powers that have been at play in the Universe since its first moment. And since we are made of the same stuff, these powers flow through us as well.

Five examples he names are:

1. Allurement – the power of attraction, how things hold together – from atoms to human love.

2. Emergence – the power of creativity, how the Universe transcends itself, and we share in this

3. Synergy – the power of working together, mutually enhancing relationships. We know the power of community.

4. Transformation – the power to change the whole, communion and intimacy. We offer ourselves for transformation to be more in tune with the Cosmos, (with what I and others call God).

5. Interrelatedness – the power of care, how the Universe responds to the other. (And so how we allow compassion to grow within us as we travel the Jesus Way.)

Taken together love, creativity, self-transcendence, cooperation, the power to change, compassion, interdependence are among our best human values or powers. We have recognised and named these powers or values, but we didn't actually invent them. They have come to us through the evolution process, because the Universe or the Cosmic Christ-Sophia is at work in and through us too. When we live in harmony with these powers or values, we care for the earth and all it contains. I understand God as this loving force field within which, as Tillich said, 'We live and move and have our being.'

All this magnificence, and yet – we struggle, we mess up, we cause ourselves and others pain and damage. There are billions of our sisters and brothers for whom daily life is simply too hard to have any energy for reflecting. We thought we all had free will and the full power to choose a better path. But it doesn't work out like that.

The ancients came up with the story of Adam and Eve to explain why it's all so hard. Later, Augustine had the idea of their 'sin' being bequeathed to us all in the form of Original Sin. We've moved on from that. Nonetheless intergenerational problems and tendencies are a reality. Some years ago there was a speaker here at St Andrew's who named the problem Original Wound, rather than Original Sin, on the grounds that we have all had imperfect (i.e. human) parents who bequeathed issues to us, and we in turn passed these or others on to our children. As a wise woman taught me, unskilled behaviour, my own and that of others, comes from these wounds of ours. Each generation is responsible for seeing to its own healing as our contribution to world peace. This is where God's offering of hope and healing comes in, the unconditional love and all-embracing compassion. As we open to receiving these gifts, so we are more able to give them to ourselves and offer them to others.

For a moment, look again at your hand, your skin – and at your neighbour's Acknowledge the magnificence of together being part of the Universe's evolutionary story. And acknowledge the magnificence, flawed and all as it is, of your unique personal inner life and your existence as a beautiful member of the species Humanity. We are One! All is One! And we must play our part in harmony with the Oneness, with the Web, with the God of our understanding.

Good Friday

> For this Good Friday service, we were invited to offer a reflection based on one of the people in the Passion story.

Mary, I've come to be with you. I can only begin to imagine what it was like for you to meet your precious son as he was carrying his cross, then to see and hear the hammering and the jolting, and now be waiting here for him to get to the end of the pain. I haven't had to watch any of my sons suffer and die. There are others here who do know what that is like.

You, Mary Magdalene and the other women are there supporting each other, each with your own particular grief. But you are the only one who spent nine months carrying him after that memorable conception. You are the only one who spent your own body and blood to give birth to him. Are you remembering the old man Simeon prophesying that a sword of sorrow would pierce your heart? This is it! That was the occasion you took your baby to be circumcised. His first bloodshed. Mothers have always found that surgical ritual hard. As he grew, there would be more – grazed knees from tumbles, cut fingers as he learned to use tools in the workshop with Joseph, maybe a bloodied nose from a neighbourhood tiff. But this is the final ebb.

You lost him before, when he was 12 and disappeared for those three days. A family mis-communication. Those I do know, and the agony of anxiety until the child is found. Then the confusing mix of relief and anger, and the 'Why on earth did you do that?' This present loss can have no such resolution.

He gives you and John into each other's care. That's so thoughtful – he always was. When had John returned to be with you all? He'd run off with all the others but must have had a change of heart along the way. I hope he's able to give you the support you'll need when it's all over. Sharing the pain and the memories will help you both.

When he says he is thirsty, and they give him the vinegar on the stick, maybe you're remembering that wedding where you asked him to help the couple with the embarrassing shortage of wine. And he did, with such amazing results.

And there was that time someone praised you for being his mother. Some took it as a put-down to you when he replied that all those who hear God's Word are mother and brothers to him. I'm sure you smiled at that, because you both knew that God's Word is deeply rooted in your life too.

You are joining the sisterhood of all those women who have lost their sons to violence at the hands of other mothers' sons. It has been happening since human time began. It happens still. I am grateful every day that my sons have not had to go and kill the sons of other mothers. They are a very privileged generation, one of the few in human history.

Mary, you have no way to imagine what will happen after this. But I like to think that as the first Easter dawns, before anything and anyone else, he will come to you, his mother, to speak of Resurrection, of new life, new hope, new power and new joy!

New Year Reflection, 2017

Now I invite you to shift focus gently from the hard, outer world of current tragedies, to our own inner world of myth and metaphor. It is equally real and also in need of our compassionate attention. Each week since the first Sunday in Advent we have sung about Jesus being born in us, which is in you and me. Today we're pondering the words of Meister Eckhart, 'Of what use is Christmas if he be not born in me?' Eckhart was a 13th century mystic, a priest-teacher of theology, whose writings were so imbued with myth and metaphor that he was scheduled for a heresy trial – but died before it could take place. His writings are now loved by many Christians.

A friend and I offered this service and blended our themes. Hers was the current outer world, refugees and new Herods. Mine was recognising the inner on-going story of Christmas.

Christmas was last week. Looking through one window, there can be sighs of relief – that's it over for another year! Through another, it's not at all over and done with. As we now move on into the New Year, how can we integrate the Christmas concept or conception of a birth taking place within us, and take that forward with us?

The idea of divinity within each of us may seem strange. Perhaps as strange as the dream message about Mary's pregnancy seemed to Joseph. While in the story he knew its conception had nothing to do with him, he was still told to adopt and nurture the Child. So no, he wasn't to put Mary away to spare her publicity.

My children had a book of Bible stories. One had a scene in the carpenter's shop. Mary came in and said, 'Joseph, we're getting a big surprise: I'm going to have a baby.' Joseph was so startled he cut his finger. 'Oh dear,' said Mary, 'I'll put a plaster on it.' In adult terms he really was in a quandary. If he respectfully 'put Mary away', he'd probably be accused when the pregnancy became obvious of not honouring his responsibility for this ex-nuptial birth. If he obeyed the angel and took her into his home, it could be seen as an admission that they had had intercourse before it was permitted. No wonder he was troubled. But he followed the angelic dream and the other guidance dreams that came to him. Such dreams still sometimes come to us – but that's a different exploration. Joseph whole-heartedly fulfilled the role of loving parent to the child, as protector, provider of homes, anxious seeker when Jesus was lost, and carpentry tutor.

How can Joseph's example support us when we have doubts about the gestation and birth of the Divine Child within ourselves? When we think of the possibility, the nurture and growth of divinity in ourselves, have we like Joseph ever been tempted to abandon this Divine Child? The whole idea can seem weird, and unreal. Accepting the possibility whole-heartedly isn't logical. What would it do to our normal lives in the world? It can be disconcerting to ponder yourself as pregnant by the Spirit. The seed of God is within us, since our lives began as innocent babies. As Eckhart says, the seeds of the pear and hazel tree grow into the next generation of their trees, so with the seed of God in us. Given due nurture, it grows us into God, into recognising that, as the Quakers say, there is that of God in everyone, including ourselves.

Maybe being pregnant with divinity is not as extraordinary as it sounds. Maybe it's another metaphor for grace, received and acted on – or the indwelling Spirit – or our goodness, our Godded-ness – or renewal of commitment to our core values, or at its simplest, growth in our ability to love. Maybe we can respond consciously and actively, and recognise, own and nurture this Life within us, growing in loving respect for ourselves, others and all Creation. Being increasingly able to convey 'I see you and you matter.' Putting ego aside makes it simpler to allow the emptying of the inner space and attend to the development of this miraculous pregnancy within us. Then we can labour with others towards the birth of the Jesus world of Love and of Peace based on Truth and Justice. If Paul could say in Galatians 2, 'It is no longer I who live, but Christ who lives in me', are we able to aim gently towards this for ourselves? This can be our own here-and-now contribution to world peace.

Light

> For a summer service.

For sunlight, starlight, moonlight
For firelight, torchlight and nightlights
For fireworks, street lights and solar panels
For matches, and light-sticks
We give thanks

For headlights, tail lights and lights in the boot
For porch lights that welcome
For candles on cakes, in church and for power cuts
For Christmas lights and flashing ear-rings
We give thanks

For lights that hatch and lights that heal
For searchlights and lighthouses
For day-light saving and long warm evenings
For light in eyes that twinkle, warm, reassure
We give thanks

For 'seeing the light', enlightenment and transformation
For feeling lighter when a burden is shared
For the warmth that accompanies light
For the light of love
We give thanks. Amen.

Ponderings

Ponderings

In this final section, I return to the quilt metaphor. The patches have now all been sorted, assembled into a pattern and stitched together. They are the top layer. The batting, the warm middle layer of a quilt, is the Gospel, the Good News that I am loved, that we all are loved and are to love each other. We all matter. I think of these last half dozen pieces as the backing and binding, finishing off the quilt, ready to be given as a gift to you, the reader.

There will be more learning and growing in the years that are left to me. Genetically speaking, I may last well into my nineties, as older generations have done. Or not. I have been decluttering my home and passing heirlooms to the younger generations, shredding, recycling papers or entrusting them to safe keeping. I've sorted and distributed my late parents' enormous photo collection and some of mine. And made the lists. It's all in hand, needed maybe tomorrow, or in 20 years' time.

Gratitude for what has been and the lessons therefrom, gratitude for what is, and for what is to come. For the peace, which when ruffled is soon restored. For the God of my understanding and Her love. For poor beautiful Earth – may we work to rescue Her from our current threats to Her well-being.

Jesus and Evolution

Trying to fit jigsaw pieces together

Now that theology and science have finally been engaging in some constructive conversation, the concept of evolution has been normalised in most Christian contexts. This needed a much-enlarged understanding from the 17th century days when it was possible to calculate the date of Creation as 23 October 4004 BC by counting the number of generations in the Gospel genealogies. Geology and palaeontology painfully sorted that out. In the same way, advances in cosmology have hugely expanded the human concepts of God, earth and the heavens, and have considerably diminished concepts of the role and centrality of human beings in the vastness of Creation. Personally, as a teenager I figured that there was no conflict between science and religion, between evolution and Creation. Scientists and theologians were all seekers after Truth. They just described it in different literary modes. Scientists, I decided, wrote newspaper articles, and the author of Genesis and theologians wrote poems. Different, but both true. And fascinatingly, the order of Creation in Genesis is virtually identical with the scientific evolutionary model.

Theology tells us that the coming of Jesus into the world changed everything. It even, for many planetary inhabitants, has divided history in two. This poem of UA Fanthorpe's has it in a nutshell:

BC–AD
This was the moment when Before
Turned into After, and the future's
Uninvented timekeepers presented arms.
This was the moment when nothing
Happened. Only dull peace
Sprawled boringly over the earth.
This was the moment when even energetic Romans
Could find nothing better to do
Than counting heads in remote provinces.
And this was the moment
When a few farm workers and three
Members of an obscure Persian sect
Walked haphazard by starlight straight
Into the kingdom of heaven.

If this birth, life and death has been of such human spiritual significance, surely it must have an evolutionary meaning. How did the birth of this Godded Man affect the development of homo sapiens? Millennia before that first Christmas, humans had become differentiated from their closest relatives, had passed from being hunter-gatherers, become agrarian, developed from tribes to peoples, combined to build cities, invented writing and science, adopted patriarchal methodology and power struggles and waged wars. Along the way, their awe had become religious as the elements and the struggle for survival had led to acknowledgement of powers beyond their own. There were the tribal wise women or men, the shamans, the healers, the seers who on behalf of their people had strong connections with the Unseen Reality, however they imaged, imagined and named that.

Then came the roots of wider religious systems, Hinduism about 4000BC and its offshoot Buddhism. Buddha was born around 463BC. The wisdom he brought to the world was a way to personal freedom from suffering, to happiness, to enlightenment. Compassion and karma are key concepts, the multiple re-births at differently-merited levels of creaturely life.

Then came Jesus. There has been an interesting comparison of the sayings of Buddha and Jesus – so many parallels.[44] And the interesting question: might Jesus have been influenced by one or more of the travelling Buddhist teachers?

What did Jesus say and do uniquely that offered a change, a development in human consciousness? He reprioritised human values by turning power structures on their head, promising those at the bottom of the heap first right of entry to the basileia, the kin-dom of heaven, or as a friend put it, the eco-system of God. His Beatitudes are the passport: blessed are the poor in spirit, those who mourn, the meek, those hungry for righteousness, the merciful, the pure in heart, the peace-makers, the persecuted, and those ostracised for their relationship with him. A list to confront, to appal even, those with 'normal' human urges to achieve their own well-being and power.

He emphasised human connectedness with all other humans and with God. His image in John's Gospel of himself as the vine and the rest of us as the branches offers a striking new image of human connectedness. Each of us is a cell in an alive, growing, greater organism. He connected with the deep need of all human beings, especially the poor, to know they are of some significance. So many individuals experienced his 'I see you and you matter', along with the personal loving-kindness they needed. And his articulation of the reciprocal reality that our feeding the hungry, welcoming strangers, clothing the naked, visiting the sick and imprisoned is giving service to the supreme Lover.

Jesus too offers 'enlightenment', transformation leading to a place of deep peace. 'Eternal life is now', being 'born of Spirit', the personal healing, the being known and loved. And a transformed understanding of power – it is to be used 'for' not 'over', in service of those with less.

Discovering these evolutionary possibilities in our own being for the benefit of the world takes commitment, time and prayer. His life and death are the template for our own repeating cycles of crucifixions, bewilderment and resurrections. Following his Way can lead each of us to evolve as human beings and contribute to our evolving societies and wider humanity.

Musings on Metaphors

A Refresh topic[57]

Augustine is supposed to have said that all language about God is metaphor. On reflection, this seems self-evident: no words can 'capture' the One beyond words. The Bible is, amongst other things, a compendium of metaphors to help us understand differing aspects or modes of the Holy One. With metaphors, there's always both the 'Is like this' and the 'Is not like this'. And words are themselves metaphors – if we think of a four-legged creature that moos and gives milk, the reality of its being is not affected by whether it is named in the various European languages as cow, vache, kuh, mucca etc. The words point to the reality of the animal, but do not share its identity. And so, it is with the Holy One, the Divine Presence: namings and their variety do not affect the Ultimate Reality.

There's a growing understanding among Christian people of faith that the Divine Presence is at work in and through all that is, and there is an essential unity, a real connectedness of All that Is: panentheism – 'God in everything'. Not pantheism, the more limiting 'God is everything'. This pervading Presence is the perspective that many Eastern and indigenous faiths never lost. The ancient symbol of the net of Indra is a beautiful image for this connectedness – All-That-Is as one net with, at each joint, a multifaceted jewel which reflects all the other jewels. Everything is present everywhere!

The same concept is supported by the newer Western scientific perspective: I've recently come across these words from the quantum physicist David Bohm:

> In the enfolded [or implicate] order, space and time are no longer the dominant factors determining the relationships of dependence or independence of different elements. Rather, an entirely different sort of basic connection of elements is possible, from which our ordinary notions of space and time, along with those of separately existent material particles, are abstracted as forms derived from the deeper order. These ordinary notions in fact appear in what is called the "explicate" or "unfolded" order, which is a special and distinguished form contained within the general totality of all the implicate orders.[45]

And he writes of the world – and us, and everything – as being holograms, each fragment containing everything. Despite the limited small picture information provided to us in daily life by our senses and ordinary experience, there is this bigger picture of unity whose existence can now be discerned scientifically.

What if his understanding of these orders (deeper, implicate and ordinary, explicate) is simply another way to describe the Mystery we call the Divine? The convergence of scientific and spiritual realities and language? The scientific discovery of the physical manifestation of the spiritual reality we have already known? Much as Teilhard de Chardin's noosphere concept of the 1920s – an envelope of human consciousness surrounding the geosphere and biosphere – has been given a 'physical' reality with the advent of the internet.

And then I met an extraordinary and exciting visible metaphor for Bohm's explicate (obvious, discernible) and implicate (deep, invisible) orders, which essentially equates to the paradox of senses and faith. Do try this at home!

Take a strip of paper that is about 3cm wide and about 25-30cm long. Give one end a half twist, then join the ends with tape or staple. You have just made a Möbius strip, a fascinating mathematical oddity discovered by August Möbius in 1858. It is a paradoxical one-sided solid – prove this to yourself by running a finger or drawing a line along the centre of the strip: you will traverse twice the length of the original strip and arrive back where you started. It does indeed have only one side! Now focus on a short section of the strip. Hold it between your index finger and thumb. Your eyes and sense of touch tell you quite clearly that the paper has two sides. But then focusing back on the larger reality of the whole construction, you have already ascertained that it has only one side! Your 'small picture' sense information has proved inadequate to give you the full truth of the bigger picture.

The world of sense is so limited. And so often we act and think as though our small picture sense information is all there is. Faith calls us to the acceptance and knowledge of the larger reality, where we are part of this amazing whole, where quite literally, no one and nothing is ever separated from the loving energy of the Holy Presence. While in faith we 'know' intellectually nothing can separate us from the love of God (Romans 8), there's the paradox of the all-too-real sense of separateness and sometimes alienation we feel from each other and from the Divine One. How can these be reconciled? The One Body of St Paul, the Vine and the Branches of Jesus! And not just the knowledge, as of an interesting but esoteric fact, but an ongoing awareness to be lived into daily life and mindfully.

Here with that little scrap of paper formed into a Möbius strip is a physical demonstration of what Brian Swimme, in his lecture series of the same name, calls the Powers of the Universe which move through all that is and has ever been. The Oneness of it All. And doesn't St Paul say essentially the same thing?

> Neither death nor life, no angel, no prince, nothing that exists, nothing still to come, not any power, or height or depth, nor any created thing can ever come between us and the love of God made visible in Christ Jesus our Lord. Romans 8:38-39.

The entire Cosmos is one fabric, one whole, of which we are all visible manifestations. All is One.

Letting Go

A *Refresh* topic[58]

Life is about letting go. So many life stages, so much pain in the letting go – sometimes a choice, but often not. And then the new freedoms, but the work of living into them.

We let go of our security in the womb to be born. We let go of the support of the sofa to stand and walk alone. We let go of parents to a greater or lesser degree through childhood and adolescence, leave home and bond with a partner. We may willingly, or not, let go of our freedom in many respects and have children. Pregnancy, birth and 20 or so years of child-rearing mean letting go of so much. Even the choice to continue a career involves letting go a precious baby or small child into the care of someone else. Then letting them go free to make their own lives is a further birth-giving. They may or may not come back or stay close. Letting go of dreams along the adult journey. Letting go of health and autonomy as old age approaches. Then the letting go of death itself.

As I think back over my own major lettings go, I am aware of the God-Presence in Jesus, my life-companion. Always there, if not necessarily in a way that was obvious to me at the time. We emigrated to New Zealand when I was nine. No choice there, grief and major adjustments in the days before children were meant to have emotional struggles. Jesus in church and Eucharist was about the only familiar experience in this new place half a world away.

In middle adulthood I learned a great deal about letting go during my time in Al-Anon, the 12-step programme for friends and families of alcoholics. Step 1: recognising that I am powerless over the alcoholic. Efforts to control their drinking are fruitless, wearing, and can usefully stop! And the wider corollary: trying to control anyone else's life beyond my own is not only fruitless, but unloving, disrespectful and counter-productive. There's the slogan 'Let go and let God'. I cannot manage the outcomes of problems or chosen courses of action. There will always be the unknown imponderables I can't possibly take into account when setting off on a course of action. Another slogan 'Detach with love' points to a way between caring too much and choosing to care no longer.

> The Serenity Prayer: God, grant me the serenity to accept the things I cannot change, the courage to change the things I can, and the wisdom to know the difference.

I discovered the key role played by the final clause: letting go the conviction that I was the best arbiter of what could and couldn't change. This led to some astonishments as circumstances reframed themselves around me. Then came the need to take responsibility for changing what could in fact be changed. Eventually the serenity crept in, once I could let go into the hands of a loving God all that was genuinely outside my ability to control.

Another major set of lettings-go came in later adulthood with the God-and-faith-and-Church journey. My physical health was suffering as I fought to reconcile the Spirit movements within with the ways of the church I had grown up in, learned so much from, and loved so deeply. Each Sunday became an ordeal as the images of the Holy One coming to birth in me conflicted almost violently with the language and imagery of the language in the service. What would leaving mean? Letting go of the Eucharist that had been my food since I was small. Letting go of a community I was fond of, though a recent house-move meant I didn't have the depth of attachment that I'd had to my previous fellow-parishioners. Letting go of the fear that rejecting the familiar words, the authority, and some of the teachings would be to set myself up as 'prideful'. Thankfully, I had no fear of eternal damnation, but this can be a challenge to others in similar circumstances. Trusting that Jesus, the Compassion of God, would lead, teach and keep me on track. John 16:13 became very important: When the Spirit of truth comes, he will lead you to the complete truth. 'Yes, but what if…?' 'Trust, love and be loved!' And Galatians 5:16: If you are guided by the Spirit, you will be in no danger of yielding to self-indulgence.

Challenges land in our laps that invite us to let go our complete-looking understandings of God and church. Do we choose to dismantle our tidy jigsaws, and incorporate new experiences, insights and understandings? Simply rejecting new concepts and information to preserve the familiar is to court stagnation.

After times of bewilderment, I eventually let go the striving to find God, and found it was replaced by the recognitions and the joys. God has always been right here, simply waiting for my eyes to let go of their scales. Discovering myself as fish in the Ocean of Love. Eucharist too has been there all the time, simply waiting to be recognised once I had torn myself away from the realities of the ritual. Ritual has always pointed to real life. Eucharist is there when I share lives over coffee with a friend, an ice-cream with a grandchild, when a mental health client offers to share a sandwich, when a counselling client or spiritual directee breaks open their life-story to my privileged hearing, when I open myself heart, mind, body and soul to the love of the One.

Now with approaching aging, I'm nearing the other necessary releasings likely or inevitable over the next couple of decades. Health – I watch carefully now those friends who are in pain and still manage to be cheerful givers and receivers of love – how do they do it? I've never been patient with pain. My role in the active world, and ability to support others through their pain. The treasures of a lifetime, not numerous, but much loved. My precious house, where solitude, peace and the view of the harbour and mountains are a constant joy. Will I be pruned from here to a bed-sit with a view of a brick wall? Conversely, I hope and pray relationships with family and friends endure and deepen. But how many of my tribe of beautiful grandchildren will I see grow to adulthood? Dying doesn't seem a problem, but the getting there might be. Can I trust the Love of my life to be beside me for that journey too? My mind says yes, but my heart isn't so sure. All I can do is pray for what I will need to walk peacefully into the final letting go, trusting that all will indeed be well.

Bad Back

This week I've learned important things
that pain eats brain cells
that it's wearing to plan every move
that I'd never appreciated easy getting
in or out of bed
Now it's an ordeal –
knees together, draw them up
roll onto side
feet onto floor and sit up
in one smooth – ow! – movement.
Plan trips to loo well ahead
and no, I can't reach behind me
to push the flush button

I have left the ranks of
the temporarily able-bodied
and joined the ranks of those
who have to ask for help
It arrives – bless the givers!

Amusements arrive too
like the morning I spilt the yoghurt
then dropped the soap-powder box on
the floor
pondered a porridge
appreciating that slow is also
meditative.

Sky theatre of birds and clouds
starlings contorting through the hole
in next door's eaves
at dawn one's beak suddenly
glowed a wondrous gold
reflecting light of rising sun.

Time to pray but can't
the noticing will have to do.
accepting 'this is how it is'
saves one layer of pain
and helps the body heal

Unaccustomed disability, fortunately temporary, but foreshadowing the serious physical aging I've so far not had to deal with.

Then thanks to experts with healing hands
the first pain-free hour
the possibility of sleep
joyful distraction of a good book
pain permitting some sedentary creativity
brief visits to computer – essentials only
slow walks from sofa to chair and back
so I don't get cast
Friends calling my pace 'majestic'
I called it decrepitude.

In less excruciating moments
pondering that many live
with constant pain like this
these curtailments of mobility
I salute them!
but relief that mine will soon be gone

I have survived
healing day by day
gratitude for
the prospect of driving
a decent walk
hanging out the washing
Remembering how it's been
will enrich the joy!

Mortality

A *Refresh* topic [59]

'It is statistically proven that ten out of ten people die!' Thus was introduced a TV ad a few decades back, sponsored by an evangelical church to encourage viewers to reflect on their lives and preparations for the inevitable Judgement and afterlife. Did it have any of the desired effect? Who knows!

During a season as chaplain in a hospice, I was surprised to find Christians who were terrified of dying in case they 'hadn't done enough' to get into heaven, and conversely, those who had worked their way to an atheistic certainty that death was their complete end and were dying with the calm of integrity. And of course, every shade of expectation and response in between. Then there were the differing belief systems of the various faith traditions. All food for thought and theological reflection.

There are many Life after Life stories of people who were clinically dead and had encounters with the Loving Light before being 'sent back' to live on. To me they ring true, even while I question the details of the experience that I – we all – will have.

When I want to get specific, I have found healing in the stories of people who in the presence of the Loving Light become fully aware of their short-comings and the effects of their actions on others. That makes it easier for me to be at peace, to reconcile with the dead ones who harmed me, now that they 'get it' and understand the effects they had on my life. Then too, in my turn, I will understand the impacts on others of my own behaviours, of which I may well be now still ignorant. Is that, minus the flames, the healing process Catholics used to call Purgatory? I was moved by someone who works in mental health saying she believed there is a special part of heaven for those who have taken their own lives: 'They need so much extra love and healing before they're ready to join the rest.'

I attended a funeral decades ago when I was pregnant, and suddenly saw the people gathered there as a body giving birth to our friend. Her physical remains were the placenta, of no further use now that she had been released into a new freer life. The 'labour' for her family and community had been hard and long, and there was relief as well as sadness now that it was over. And recently I learned a new designation – death doula – for a person who accompanies another through their final illness as a primary support and 'midwife' for the process of dying. It's a privileged role I've had for several friends.

A US therapist Phyllis Silverman talked about continuing bonds with those who have died. The relationships, whatever their quality, continue and can continue to develop. This is far truer to lived experience than 'closure' and 'getting over it'. So many of us do have ongoing conversations with our departed ones!

I can vouch for both the continued development of relationship and the enlightenment that comes through dying. Many years ago, when I was on retreat the spiritual director was firmly recommending that I go with Jesus to meet my husband who had died suddenly several years previously. I was reluctant, but dutifully began the imagining. Then I was astounded by the interactions between the three of us and was re-made by the reconciliation that came about. There was a total healing I likened to heart surgery. I'd no idea I needed that, or that my husband would be a healed compassionate self. And I hope my children, grandchildren and friends will still have chats with me when I'm no longer on earth.

We live in faith in a loving God for the hereafter. But all that is beyond our current grounded day-to-day experience. In the here and now there are practical steps we can take to prepare ourselves for the distant – or possibly not – day of our own death. There is a Buddhist meditation where the invitation is to visualise one's self in the casket, and the funeral which will be held. And then to visualise the disintegration of our body. When this can be experienced fully, there is a deepened appreciation of being alive now, of our connection to those we love.

Practical preparations are in order, as an act of love for family members and others. Is there an up-to-date will? Signed-up Powers of Attorney for care of our well-being and medical treatments and property? An Advance Directive on Treatment Decisions? What about planning your funeral service? I planned mine 30 years ago when I was first widowed, and I knew my children wouldn't have a clue where to start should mine occur at that stage. It has been revised multiple times since then in terms of context, theology, language and people, and is there for my family to work with when the time comes. They know how to access this information. It is never too early to make these preparations. And from Juliet Batten's *Spirited Ageing*, I delightedly adopted the suggestion of compiling a list of music I'd like to die to. My family has this list and when the time comes will play me the beloved melodies from the classics.

At a recent workshop entitled 'What makes a Good Death?' we were all asked to identify factors that would make for a good death for ourselves. Most opted for freedom from pain, harmony in relationships, lack of extended disability, time to prepare, choices around accepting treatment or not, and a loving and respectful context. These may or may not all be possible. I know that hospice care maximises what is possible. For some their capacity to choose the moment was important. This complex question is too big to do more than mention here, other than to say there's a strong but not universal Christian strand of resistance to voluntary euthanasia. Even the definition is open to a range of interpretations.

Then what happens? Scientific advances in cosmology have of necessity modified both our theology and our spiritual geography. We can no longer envisage heaven or God as 'up there'. So where and how we will be in God and with God has become more of a mystery. But what I know for sure is that Divine Love goes on, that there are dimensions beyond space-time, and – somehow – we become part of All That Is. Alleluia!

Am I a Christian?

A recent discussion offered the question 'What do I say if I'm asked whether I'm a Christian?' After much reflection, here is my response, which summarises some of the important threads of this book.

Whatever an enquirer's definition of 'Christian', I am unlikely to match it. I certainly can't assent to the traditional evangelical shibboleth 'Do you believe that God the Father sent His Son Jesus to die for our sins?' No, no and no. No male God, no 'sending' and no 'dying for our sins'. And no 'sins' either. That word has been deleted from my vocabulary for individuals, but not for institutions. I have taken to heart my 'non-spiritual' psychotherapist's wisdom 'All unskilled behaviour comes out of wounds.' It is the most profoundly compassionate statement I have met. I know its truth for myself and hold it for everyone else.

For the Religion question of the 2019 Census, I wrote Christian, post-denominational. The ecclesiastical institutions I have known most closely have grown such an overlay of regulations which frequently trump the basic Gospel message that I no longer want a label. The Gospel of inclusivity and equality is preached, but the contradictions between that and actual church rules are hardly noticed by most parishioners.

The 8 Points of Progressive Christianity (2020) work well enough for me. Point 1 says,

> '…following the path of the teacher Jesus can lead to healing and wholeness, a mystical connection to 'God', as well as an awareness and experience of not only the Sacred, but the Oneness and Unity of all life.'

My alignment with this is based on my relationship with Jesus. As already related, this began when I was six, and has, since then, been the axle on which my life turns. It began with a Catholic child's prayer-book which had Jesus telling the Gospel stories from his own point of view, and assuring the child of his desire to hear her/his stories and concerns. It was about being loved and listened to. I was a literal-minded child, so later when I met the primary commandment of both Hebrew and Christian Scriptures: 'Love God with your whole heart, mind and strength,' I wondered how to go about loving God. The answer – 'If you love me, keep my commandments.' So that became the aim, from love – nothing at all about guilt or punishment!

That first Point mentions experience of the sacred. From the mid-1980s for a decade, I had that series of astonishing and healing encounters with Jesus. There are, I discovered, people with a particular inborn personality type/brain structure who are likelier to have spiritual experiences and contact with archetypal material. I know now that All is One, that absolutely everything is permeated by the Divine. In the seasons of poverty, I learned through other surprising experiences that when I'd done my utmost, my material needs would be met. And yes, I wonder why me, when so many others suffer so much? I'm deeply, deeply appreciative of all that. All those experiences and their lessons have had to be integrated alongside my questioning and thinking. I have discarded most of the traditional dogmas and doctrines, particularly the Atonement theology of the death of Jesus. This was thought through in *Exploring the Presence* (EP 115).

Spiritual direction has been crucial to the journey and I am grateful for the personal guidance and companionship of some very wise people. Prayer has changed through the different seasons of life. Now it is more likely to be a simple 'being with' meditation, an acknowledgement of Divine Presence in everything, listening attention, and conversations with Jesus along the way in everyday life.

There is this all-Encompassing, all-Permeating, loving and responsive ultimate reality. These days, I understand 'God' as process, rather than entity, a loving, intelligent, responsive process. This can also be called Spirit, Cosmic Christ, Life-Force, the Universe, Evolution, Creative Energy, Allah, Brahman, Atman, Love, the qi and li of Neo-Confucianism, Deepest Truth and more. Learning to live in tune with this Ultimate Reality makes sense of human life. The wisdom of past generations gives us the guidelines for doing so – Love, Truth, Justice, Peace, Compassion and Service. The meaning and purpose of human life is to learn to love – Holy Mystery, Self and Others.

Science in the 21st century acknowledges mystery, the fluidity of material, the expanding cosmos with its unfathomable distances and glories. Its observable powers and values have passed through the aeons into the latest products of Evolution, into us human beings. Dark Energy and Dark Matter are acknowledged as existing but are shrouded in mystery. Might they have some close God-connection? What if the Big Bang was the explosive release of Loving Creativity? That would be congruent with my understanding of God, the Power, the Spirit that exists in everything.

It is good that Christian attention on the spiritual life is being diverted from being solely geared to attaining a blessed after-life, towards attending to self, each other and the planet, the coming of the kin-dom now. This has led to parts of Christianity merging with what is known as the Secular Age. For me, there is no sacred/secular dichotomy. All is sacred. But even in the so-called secular world there is a human thirst for, and experience of, the Beyond which can lead to a re-enchantment of the human journey. We need not do the dualistic either/or, rationality or spirituality. It has to be both. Maybe this realisation will bring us to a new age that might become known as Neo-Christianity. Dedication to both the inner spiritual journey and to the external journey of loving service, all enlarged by integration of new scientific truths. That's how it was always meant to be!

The Commandments of God in the Biblical faith traditions are meant to harmonise us with all else that is as the way to live, descriptive – rather than prescriptive – of good community relationships. We are in community with all other creatures on Earth, and with Earth Herself. I see Her as God's body, the embodying of the Divine. Now this Earth is screaming painfully and very loudly 'If you love me, keep my commandments'. We are having to hear this, digest it and take action, because we already taste the hell of climate change catastrophe that awaits if we do not obey. Consequences, not punishment!

All Faiths are culturally-generated systems of Myth, symbols and metaphors which endeavour to teach us those life-lessons. We are probably born into the Myth of our own culture and may supplement it with wisdom learned from the others. When the whole of life turns on the axle of our Myth, when we immerse ourselves deeply in living its ways, it will come alive for us in ways that astonish and guide. Deep living of our Myth brings ordeal, resolution and eventually great joy and peace. We will know ourselves as Beloved and as one with All that Is. There is then no need to 'seek God', to 'find God'. All that is necessary is to 'recognise God' in every scintilla of everything – in atoms, in cells, in our own being and in All That Is.

My Myth is relationship with the Divine through Jesus. It is impossible for this relationship to be a private piety. Involvement in social justice is its necessary corollary. Recognising and serving him in others. Working for peace based on Gospel justice.

Being unsurprised when that leads to opposition. Learning from marginalised people lessons of courage, resilience and humility. Learning to love as I am loved. And spending daily times, however brief, renewing awareness of the Love.

I feel huge gratitude for the treasures, and no less for the excruciating times of life. Without them, I would not have learned what I now know from experience: God is faithful, God is Love! I live with a deep well of peace. Nothing of this prevents or magics away pain and concerns. I mess up and get hurt often enough. But I've learned not to worry, to hold or reclaim my serenity, and to trust that All Will Be Well.

It's so challenging, yet so simple: Love one another as I have loved you!

Blessing

I wish you
Peace that can be kept
Love that can be given
Joy that can be shared
And the grace to receive

Endnotes

1. Dennis Klass, Phyllis R. Silverman, Steven L. Nickman, *Continuing Bonds: New Understandings of Grief,* (Taylor & Francis, Abingdon 1996)
2. https://acsd.org.nz/, https://www.sdicompanions.org/
3. Andrew Newberg & Mark Robert Waldman, *How God Changes your Brain* (Ballantine Books, New York, 2009)
4. Wade, Jenny, *Changes of Mind: A Holonomic Theory of the Evolution of Consciousness,* SUNY NY, 1996
5. Brian Swimme, *The Powers of the Universe: an exploration of the powers coursing through the universe and each of us.* 3 DVDs. (Center for the Story of the Universe, Mill Valley, CA, 2004)
6. Arvo Pärt, *Alina* (ECM 1591, Frankfurt 1999)
7. http://www.herchurch.org/.
8. Sisters of St Joseph, Archives.
9. https://uscatholic.org/news_item/liberation-theology-finds-new-welcome-in-pope-francis-vatican/
10. Personal communication, March 26, 2013
11. Sisters of St Joseph, Archives.
12. *Evening Post*, 10 December 1991
13. Personal communication, 27 March 2013
14. Presbyterian Church of New Zealand. Overtures to the General Assembly of 2 November, 1991.
15. Further reading: David Bromell, Felix Donnelly, Willem Hein and Rosemary Neave, *Love Unbounded: on being gay or lesbian and Christian*, Colcom Press, Hibiscus Coast, NZ, 1991.

    Trish McBride, *Faith Evolving: A Patchwork Journey*, P. McBride, Wellington, 2005, 91-95, 113-115, 124-126.
16. Shirley Erena Murray, quoted with permission. *Faith Forever Singing*, NZ Hymnbook Trust Palmerston North, 2000
17. Finance, Industrial (Textile and Wood) Retail, Stores & Transport
18. *Wopsy, The Adventures of a Guardian Angel*, by Gerard F Scriven, Samuel Walker Ltd, London, 1943.
19. https://www.stuff.co.nz/entertainment/107035824/taika-waititi-says-new-zealand-is-still-racist-but-things-are-improving
20. Jojo Rabbit, 2019
21. Waldron, Vincent R & Kelley, Douglas L., *Communicating Forgiveness*, Sage Publications, Los Angeles, USA: 2008. 132
22. Taylor, A.J.W., *Justice as a Basic Human Need, New Ideas in Psychology*, 21, 3 Nov 2003. 209-219
23. Maslow, A.H., A *Theory of Human Motivation*. Psychological Review, 50(4), 1943, 370-96
24. Hermans, Judith, *Trauma and Recovery*, London, UK: Pandora, 1992. 189-90
25. The Kairos Theologians. T*he Kairos Document, Challenge to the Church*, Grand Rapids, Michigan, USA: Wm. B Eerdmans Publishing Co, 1986. 37-47.
26. Strong, James, *Expanded Edition Strong's Complete Word Study Concordance of the Bible*, AMG Publishers, Chatanooga, Tennessee, 2004.
27. Robinson, Geoffrey, *Confronting Power and Sex in the Catholic Church, Reclaiming the Spirit of Jesus*, John Garratt, Victoria, Australia, 2007. 220-225.

28 Thompson, Ann, *Say Sorry, a harrowing childhood in Catholic orphanages*, Epilogue, Thomas Doyle, Penguin, North Shore, NZ, 2009. 192-194.
29 https://progressivechristianity.org/the-8-points/
30 Webb, Val, in *Like Catching Water in a Net*
31 Karl Rahner, quoted by Rich Heffern. https://www.ncronline.org/blogs/ncr-today/call-be-mystic
32 https://seasonofcreation.com/
33 https://www.sacred-texts.com/chr/wosf/wosf22.htm
34 https://www.sbl-site.org/publications/article.aspx?ArticleId=129
35 https://www.columban.org.au/
36 All prayers from this service ©Trish McBride 2014
37 https://www.standrews.org.nz/archives/category/order-of-service
38 https://www.visitzealandia.com/Visit/the-sanctuary-valley
39 S. Murray, *Alleluia Aotearoa*, no. 26 (Palmerston North: NZ Hymnbook Trust, 1993).
40 D. Scott, *Ask That Mountain – The Story of Parihaka* (Auckland: Reed, 1975), 53.
41 C. Gibson, *Faith Forever Singing*, no. 63, (NZ Hymnbook Trust, 2004).
42 Bruce G. Sanguin, *If Darwin Prayed: Prayers for Evolutionary Mystics* (Evans and Sanguin, 2012), 143
43 S. Murray, *Alleluia Aotearoa*, no. 155
44 Jesus and Buddha, *The Parallel Sayings,* ed, Introduction Kornfield
45 Bohm, D, *Wholeness and the Implicate Order,*1980.
46 https://apod.nasa.gov/apod/archivepixFull.html
47 *Tui Motu InterIslands:* Book Review, *A Stardust Revolution*, August 2014
48 *Tui Motu InterIslands,* March 2013
49 *Tui Motu InterIslands:* November, 2014
50 *Refresh,* Vol 16, No 2, 2016
51 *Refresh, V*ol 15, No 2, 2015
52 *Tui Motu InterIslands:* May, 2015
53 *Tui Motu InterIslands:* (published as *Working for Family-Fair Wages*) Issue 228, 2018
54 *Dominion Post* 13 November 2018
55 *Tui Motu InterIslands:* (published as *A Future of Hope*) Issue 233, 2018.
56 *Presence, The Spiritual Directors International Journal*, Vol 22, No 2, 2016
57 *Refresh,* Vol 12, No 1, 2013
58 *Refresh,* Vol 14, No 1, 2015
59 *Refresh,* Vol 18, No 2, 2018

Bibliography

Adyashanti, *Resurrecting Jesus, Embodying the Spirit of a Revolutionary Mystic*, Sounds True, Boulder, 2014

Batten, Juliet, *Spirited Ageing: cultivating the art of renewal.* Ishtar Books, 2013

Berkowitz, Jacob, *The Stardust Revolution, the new story of our origin in the stars*, Prometheus, NY, 2012

Bohm, David, *Wholeness and the Implicate Order*, Routledge, Abingdon, UK 1980

Borg, Marcus, *The Heart of Christianity, Rediscovering a Life of Faith*, HarperCollins, NY, 2004

Jesus and Buddha, The Parallel Sayings, ed, Introduction Kornfield, J. Duncan Baird, London, 2008

Broomfield, John, *Other Ways of Knowing: Recharting Our Future with Ageless Wisdom*, Inner Traditions, Rochester

Corn, Seane, *Revolution of the Soul: Awaken to Love Through Raw Truth, Radical Healing, and Conscious Action*, Sounds True, Boulder, 2019

Darragh, N., ed, *Journeying into Prayer, People and their Pathways*, Accent Publications, Auckland, 2012

Living in the Planet Earth, Faith Communities and Ecology, Accent, 2014

But is it Fair? Faith communities and Social Justice, Accent, 2016

Fanthorpe, U.A., *Christmas Poems*, Enitharmon, London, 2002

Fowler, J.W., *Stages of Faith, The Psychology of Human Development and the Quest for Meaning*, San Francisco, Harper, 1995

Gateley, Edwina, *There was no Path So I Trod One*, Source Books, Trabuco, 1996

Gawande, Atul, *Being Mortal, Illness, Medicine and What Matters in the End*, Profile Books, London, 2014

Griffiths, Bede, *The Cosmic Revelation: The Hindu Way to God*, 1983

Hermans, Judith, *Trauma and Recovery*, London, UK: Pandora, 1992

Houston, Jean, Godseed, T*he Journey of Christ*, The Theosophical Publishing House, Wheaton Il, 1992

Keirsey, D. & Bates, M., P*lease Understand Me, Character and Temperament Types*, Prometheus, Del Mar CA, 1984

Kelsey, M., *Encounter with God, A Theology of Christian Experience*, Paulist Press, Mahwah NJ, 1988

Magee, Rhonda V., T*he Inner Work of Racial Justice, Healing Ourselves and Transforming our Communities Through Mindfulness*, Tarcher Perigee, NY, 2019

McBride, Trish, *Faith Evolving, A Patchwork Journey*, P. McBride, Wellington, 2005.

Exploring the Presence: More Faith Patches, Wellington, NZ: P. McBride, 2011.

Michael, CP & Norrisey, MC, *Prayer and Temperament, Different Prayer Forms for Different Personality Types*, The Open Door, Charlottesville, 1984

Murray, Shirley E., in *Faith Forever Singing*, Palmerston North, Hymnbook Trust, 2000.

Newberg, Andrew and Waldman, Mark Robert, *How God Changes your Brain*, Ballantine Books, NY, 2009

Robinson, Geoffrey. *Confronting Power and Sex in the Catholic Church, Reclaiming the Spirit of Jesus*, John Garratt, Victoria, Australia, 2007. 220-225.

Sanguin, Bruce G., *If Darwin Prayed: Prayers for Evolutionary Mystics*, Evans and Sanguin, 2012

Scott D., *Ask That Mountain – The Story of Parihaka*: Reed, Auckland, 1975

Strong, James, *Expanded Edition Strong's Complete Word Study Concordance of the Bible*, AMG Publishers, Chatanooga, Tennessee, 2004.

Swimme, Brian, *The Powers of the Universe: an exploration of the powers coursing through the universe and each of us*. 3 DVDs. Mill Valley, CA: Center for the Story of the Universe, 2004

Thompson, Ann, *Say Sorry, a harrowing childhood in Catholic orphanages*, Epilogue, Thomas Doyle, Penguin, North Shore, NZ, 2009

The Kairos Theologians, *The Kairos Document, Challenge to the Church*, Eerdmans, Grand Rapids, Michigan, 1986

Wade, Jenny, *Changes of Mind: A Holonomic Theory of the Evolution of Consciousness*, SUNY, NY, 1996

Waldron, Vincent R. & Kelley, Douglas L., *Communicating Forgiveness*, Sage Publications, Los Angeles, USA: 2008.

Webb, V., *Like Catching Water in a Net, Human attempts to Describe the Divine*, Continuum, NY, 2007

Wohlleben, Peter, *The Hidden Life of Trees: What They Feel and How They Communicate*, Greystone, Canada, 2016

Periodicals

Presence, An International Journal of Spiritual Direction, ed Wagner, N., Spiritual Directors International, Bellevue, WA

Refresh, Journal of Contemplative Spirituality, ed Gilliam-Weeks, D., Spiritual Growth Ministries Trust, Dannevirke

Tui Motu InterIslands, An Independent Catholic Magazine, ed Gilroy, A., Dunedin

Websites

Association of Christian Spiritual Directors in New Zealand:
https://acsd.org.nz/

Dorothy Walters and Andrew Harvey discuss Kundalini:
https://www.youtube.com/watch?v=CGyQnJyDDlU

herchurch:
http://www.herchurch.org/

Kairos Southern Africa:
https://kairossouthernafrica.wordpress.com/

Living Wage Movement Aotearoa New Zealand:
https://www.livingwage.org.nz/

Mahboba's Promise:
https://mahbobaspromise.org/

NASA: Astronomy Picture of the Day Archive:
https://apod.nasa.gov/apod/archivepix.html

Progressive Christianity:
https://progressivechristianity.org/the-8-points/

SDI - The Home of Spiritual Companionship:
https://www.sdicompanions.org/

Spiritual Growth Ministries Aotearoa New Zealand:
https://www.sgm.org.nz/

Spirituality & Practice:
https://www.spiritualityandpractice.com/

St Andrew's on The Terrace:
https://www.standrews.org.nz/

The National:
https://www.thenational.ae/arts-culture/books/the-great-realisation-why-this-british-writer-s-pandemic-poem-caught-the-eye-of-jake-gyllenhaal-1.1015262

Tui Motu InterIslands Magazine:
https://tuimotu.org/

Glossary

Note: The Māori language is one of the official languages of Aotearoa New Zealand. Many of these words are in use in official documents and general conversation.

Aotearoa	Land of the Long White Cloud, New Zealand
Arepa	Transliteration of Alpha
aroha	Love
Arohata	Love, Wellington Women's Prison
awhina	Support, help
Hamuera	Transliteration of Samuel
haoiho	Endangered yellow-eyed penguin
hongi	Greeting, pressing noses, exchanging breath
hui	Gathering, conversation
Iwi	Tribe
kai	Food
Kāi Tāhu	Main South Island tribe
kaitiakitanga	Guardianship of, e.g. the planet
kākā	Tree parrot
kākāriki	Red-polled small parrot
karakia	Prayer
kauri	Tree
kererū	Wood-pigeon
kia kaha	Be strong!
kia ora	Hello, thank you
koru	Furled fern shoot
kuia	Old woman
mākutu	Dark arts
mana	Dignity, status
mangai	Representative
māramatanga	World of light, illumination
Matariki	Māori New Year, the Pleiades
Mātua	Father (God the Father)
Mauī	Mythical hero
mōrehu	Survivor, remnant

moko	Women's chin tattoo
Ōmeka	Transliteration of Omega
pākehā	Non-Māori
Papatūānuku	Mother Earth, of Creation myth
Parihaka	Village invade by British troops in 1881
Rakiura	Stewart Island
Rātana	Village near Whanganui, prophet of same name
taha	Native
Tama	Son, God the Son
tangata whenua	People of the land, i.e. Māori
taonga	Treasure
tauiwi	Strangers, used as 'Others', non-Māori
te māngai	The Mouthpiece, representative
Te Ōmeka	Transliteration of Omega, the end
Te reo	The Māori language
Te Titiriti o Waitangi	The Treaty of Waitangi, 1840, between Māori and the British Government
Te Whiti	Christian convert and non-violence leader, 1870s
tohunga	Spiritual leader, scholar
tui	Bird
ture wairua	Spiritual law
ture tangata	Law of the people
wāhi tapu	Sacred place
wāhine toa	Strong women
waiata	Song
Wairua Tapu	Holy Spirit
wānanga	Place of learning
weka	Bush hen
whakapapa	Heredity, ancestry
whakawhānaungatanga	Culture of working together as family, relationships
whānau	Family, extended family
whetū Mārama	Starlight

Acknowledgements

With thanks to the people and staff of Mana Recovery and Arohata who have taught me so much. And everyone else who has shared their story with me.

This book would never have happened without the companionship and support of so many people along my life-journey. The friends, old and new, the teachers, and the spiritual directors – you all know who you are, and you may have found yourselves in these pages. In particular I'd like to thank Terry and Veronica Leamy for supportive friendship, love and loyalty through almost half a century. Thanks to Margaret Anne Mills, Anne Hadfield, Barbara Sampson, Marg Schrader, and Graham Millar for sharing the journey. Thanks to Ann Gilroy, Diane Gilliam-Weeks, Nick Wagner, and Neil Darragh, editors respectively of *Tui Motu Interislands, Refresh: Journal of Contemplative Spirituality, Presence: An International Journal of Spiritual Direction*, and the series of New Zealand theology books. Your seeing something of publishable value in my offerings over the years has been very confidence-building.

A special thanks to my friends and companions on the Way at St Andrew's on The Terrace. We are so diverse, and that is beautiful! Another fascinating patchwork!

Thanks to Philip Garside for his enormous work preparing *A Love Quilt* for publication. Skills, attention to detail, and commitment to my vision for the book have made this an affirming and educational process.

A loving and grateful acknowledgement to those important ones who have left this dimension: Columba McBride, my first encourager and best possible mother-in-law, Marlene Dunn, my first spiritual director/companion, Laura Muir, astonishingly skilled and generous psychotherapist, and Daniel O'Leary for the many lessons in humility and grace.

Arohanui,
Trish

About the Author

Trish McBride was born in Lancaster, England and came to Aotearoa New Zealand in 1952. For most of her life she was deeply involved in the Catholic Church. She has subsequently spent times with ExAlt, a women's spirituality group, a Progressive Presbyterian parish, and the Religious Society of Friends, and now identifies as post-denominational.

Now retired, Trish has been a spiritual director, chaplain in various contexts, counsellor and supervisor. She is mother to 7 and delighted grandmother to 23, some acquired, and is now (2024) happily settled in a retirement village.

A high point in her writing career was as a prize-winner in a 1994 international competition for religious journalism awarded by *The Tablet,* London. Others have been contributing chapters to five Aotearoa Catholic-based theology books, (*The God Book, A Thinkers Guide to Sin, Journeying into Prayer, But is it Fair?* and *Living in the Planet Earth*), publication of two academic papers in USA, and completing her own unintended trilogy: *Faith Evolving, Exploring the Presence* and *A Love Quilt.*

Many of the articles and poems in her books have previously appeared in a variety of publications. Formal studies included MA (Hons) in Classics, Diploma in Pastoral Ministry and Recognition as an Associate in Christian Ministry (interdenominational).

Involvements include family, social justice, nurturing friendships, quilting, reading, swimming, walking and occasional painting.

About the Book

A Love Quilt records a spirituality of aging, where many paths and truths are understood to converge. This engaging spiritual memoir quilts together 68 pieces of Trish McBride's writing from the last decade. The overall theme is that the meaning and purpose of human life is learning to love – ourselves, others, earth, cosmos, and Holy Mystery, the one of so many names. Trish believes we are all on a spiritual journey, whether or not we call it that.

Her efforts to live out her post-denominational Christianity are documented in her pieces on social justice, mental health, interfaith and racial relationships, prayer, non-orthodox theologies on forgiveness and same sex marriage, critiques of church practices, metaphor as the viable alternative to biblical literalism, and community – including her Covid-19 lock-down diary. The book also includes reflections on her travels near and far.

Praise for A Love Quilt

"Within Trish's central theme of love, come some refreshing and diverse contexts, e.g. working alongside mental health consumers; engaging with people of different faiths and ethnicities and those in our community who identify as LGBTI. We find subjects as varied as quantum physics, cosmology, ecology, evolution and interspirituality. Although social justice is the backbone of Trish's faith in action; contemplation, mysticism and playing with metaphors of the Nameless One, are also essential companions on her journey of love. I challenge you to lovingly pick up this book and be prepared to be refreshed."

Heather Sangster-Smith, Educator, Advocate, Facilitator

"This is a work of such richness and spiritual insight… Trish McBride has opened her story and her soul to her readers and enabled us all to profit from her deep understanding of her own pilgrimage. … In many ways Trish's story is so different from my own, that it was surprising and exciting to discover that her bold experiments, her deep experiences and her explorations have significant benefit even for those of us who have gone in different directions."

Peter Lineham, MNZM, Emeritus Professor of History

"A rich reading experience! This is a wonderfully multifaceted quilt – inspiring, challenging, and thought provoking. All the pieces are sewn together with the continuous thread of love."

Sheila Pritchard, Spiritual director and supervisor

"If you have wrestled with religious institutions yet have a deep desire to encounter God as Divine Love, then this book is for you. You will be challenged to become conscious of your existing language, frameworks, ideas and to move into a deep and personal encounter with Love. You will find stories that engage you and challenge you to look at your own deep story and most of all you will encounter Love."

Dr Bernadette Miles,
Co-founder and Director of Kardia Formation P/L, Australia,
Member, Coordinating Council of Spiritual Directors International

"A quilt is the perfect metaphor for this beautiful patchwork of what the author describes as 'pieces of my learning and thinking from the last decade.' As in her earlier volumes, Trish engages the reader in an intimate personal conversation about the spiritual journey."

John Broomfield, Past President, California Institute of Integral Studies

Books by Trish McBride

Trish's three books – *Faith Evolving*, *Exploring the Presence* and *A Love Quilt* – are being republished in 2024. Read together, they document Trish's 75-year life and faith journey from childhood to her 80s – a unique longitudinal record of women's spirituality and thinking. They are both spiritual biography and contextual theology.

Along the way, Trish moves from a traditional Catholic faith to embracing feminist theology and on into a post-denominational, inclusive, integrated Gospel-centred spirituality. She has used a patchwork metaphor across all three books, connecting writings of many colours, shapes and textures. Her purpose in all three has been to encourage others to ponder and record their own faith journeys.

Available in Print and as eBooks (in PDF, ePub and Kindle-Mobi formats)
Order Trish's books at: www.philipgarsidebooks.com

Faith Evolving: *A Patchwork Journey*
3rd edition – Republished – 2024

How is religious faith affected by our life's experiences? Trish McBride started with a traditional Christian faith, which evolved into a belief in a God who is free of denominational boundaries. The various 'patches' of 30 years of life-faith poems, prayers and stories have become a compelling story that will touch your heart and invite reflection.

Exploring the Presence: *More Faith Patches*
Republished – 2024

The passionate, rich and honest story of a woman who left her church after awakening to the Divine Feminine. Trish honours the Presence of the Holy One who permeates All that Is, however we may name Her / Him, in an authentic expression of women's spirituality. A fearless spiritual exploration of other ways of knowing.

A Love Quilt: *Later Faith Patches*
Republished – 2024

A compilation of later-life writings from Trish's 75-year spiritual journey, blending Christian spirituality and unorthodox ideas on matters such as love, inter-faith, race, social justice, and science. Stories, poems, and liturgies to inspire you on your journey, encourage you and provoke thoughtful reflection.

www.ingramcontent.com/pod-product-compliance
Lightning Source LLC
Chambersburg PA
CBHW081359070526
44583CB00020B/2597